THE YOUNG ABOLITIONISTS
OR,
CONVERSATIONS ON SLAVERY

THE YOUNG ABOLITIONISTS

OR,

CONVERSATIONS ON SLAVERY

By
J. ELIZABETH JONES

The Black Heritage Library Collection

 BOOKS FOR LIBRARIES PRESS
FREEPORT, NEW YORK
1971

First Published 1848
Reprinted 1971

INTERNATIONAL STANDARD BOOK NUMBER:
0-8369-8731-4

LIBRARY OF CONGRESS CATALOG CARD NUMBER:
75-138339

PRINTED IN THE UNITED STATES OF AMERICA

THE

YOUNG ABOLITIONISTS;

OR

CONVERSATIONS ON SLAVERY.

BY

J. ELIZABETH JONES.

BOSTON:

PUBLISHED AT THE ANTI-SLAVERY OFFICE.

XXI. CORNHILL.

1848.

THE YOUNG ABOLITIONISTS.

CHAPTER I.

"MOTHER! let me go to meeting too," said young Charlie Selden, who was anxious to know all that was going on.

"No, my child, you must stay at home with Phil and Jenie, and keep Biddy company."

"But I want to go and hear that man that was here to-day. You said he was going to lecture. I like *him*. We chased each other all round the old pasture, he helped me sail my boat, he played with old Tig, and it was rare sport we had. Mother, he asked me if I were an abolitionist. What did he mean? What is an abolitionist?"

"It is one who is endeavoring to liberate the slaves, my dear."

"The slaves! I heard you talking about the slaves the other day. What is a slave, Mother?"

"A slave is one who is deprived of his freedom — one who is obliged to do the bidding of a master," said the parent.

"Is Biddy a slave then? She does just what you and father tell her. She never goes out without your consent, and in every thing waits for your orders. Does this make her a slave?"

"Oh, no! Biddy, it is true, always obeys our orders, but we pay her well for her services. Every Saturday night she receives her wages and does what she pleases with them. Then Biddy is free to leave us and seek another home whenever she likes; and besides, she spends a great deal of time in reading, and writes to all her friends in old Ireland."

"Don't the slaves read and write too?" inquired Charlie.

"No, they are not permitted to learn. Their masters are afraid to have them taught, and in some States it is prohibited by law, in Louisiana, for instance."

"I know where Louisiana is very well, and on my chart I can tell by the light and dark shading which are the barbarous and which are the enlightened portions of the globe. Now I remember that the United States are all shaded very light, meaning, as my teacher says, that the people are educated. I should think Louisiana ought to be shaded very dark if they won't let the people learn. The slaves are people, mother, are they not?"

"Yes, they are men and women."

"Are the slave women just like Biddy, and the slave men like Cæsar?"

"Yes, some of them are black as Cæsar is, and some are white like Biddy," replied his mother. "Cæsar, you know, has been so unfortunate as to lose one of his ears, and several of his fingers. Sometimes the slaveholders, that is the masters, are so cruel as to cut off the ears of their slaves as a punishment for some fault; sometimes they whip them very hard and make the blood run freely; and sometimes they heat irons red hot and burn letters in their faces. Sometimes they make heavy iron collars and compel the slaves to wear them, and some have even been burned alive!"

"Oh, how horrible that is!" cried Charlie. "The slaveholders must be very cruel. Why, in the Indian wars I've read about, they didn't do worse than that! Mother, did I ever see a slave?"

" Yes, my child, you saw one the other day. Do you remember the colored man whom we met at Mrs. Walker's ?"

" Why ! is *he* a slave ? Do tell me all about him. How did he get away from his master? I guess *he* never was whipped ; he looks too bold and too strong for that."

" My dear child, the boldest and the strongest are alike powerless in the hands of a master ! They dare not resist the most severe punishment ! They have no protection from the worst of injuries !"

" But I cannot talk more with you now ; I must go to the meeting. At some future time I will tell you all you want to know about the slaves."

" Let Jenie and Phil hear too, mother. Phil is a little boy, but I'm sure he would know it was wrong to have slaves. Will Mr. Wright come here to-morrow ? He said when he came here again he would mend the mast of my boat, and I guess he could teach me to fly my kite. Mother, we never had such a visiter as Mr. Wright before."

" No, Charlie, you are quite correct in this, and at some convenient time I will tell you all about this visiter; how he loves little children, and is always teaching them to be good, and to follow peace principles."

"Does he answer all the questions children ask him? If he does, I wish we could have him for our teacher. I don't think Mr. Gardner loves children very much. He don't like to answer our questions. The other day when Jenie was reading her Bible, she asked him what it meant to 'Hide the outcast.' I suppose she was thinking something about Hide and Seek. He told her she asked quite too many questions. Mother, will you tell Jenie some time what it means to 'Hide the outcast?'"

"Yes, my dear, I shall be very happy to." With that the mother departed, and Charlie ran away to the nursery to tell Jenie and Phil what he had learned about the slaves. Jenie was a gentle little girl, very kind to her brothers, and always ready to listen to Charlie's stories. Phil was the youngest, about three years old, and a noble boy he was. He had a great head and a great heart, and his beautiful blue eyes beamed with intense interest at the simple story of the wrongs and sufferings of the slaves. He was besides a droll little fellow. All the odd

expressions he heard Biddy, or Cæsar, or anybody else use, he remembered and frequently
repeated. More than once while Charlie was
talking he exclaimed "Oh, my stars!" "Gra-
cious me!" "Saints preserve us!" and
"Charlie, if I were there, wouldn't I set Tig
on the naughty men that do such naughty
things?"

Charlie had been better instructed than to
suppose that would be right, and he endeavored
to make his brother understand the same; still
he felt that something ought to be done.

But Phil was decided in regard to the matter.
He thought the masters ought to be punished,
and he wished a good many times that he was a
man, and if he could see the slaves he would
tell them all to knock their masters down and
then run away.

In this opinion he was greatly strengthened
by Biddy, who had considerable of the war
spirit in her, and overhearing their conversation,
exclaimed —

"And sure, master Phil, ye'd be in the right
of it, the ould thieves of the world, to be after
trating a nager in that way, who is jist as good
as the best of them, and a great dale better, bad

luck to them ! I heard the blessed mister O'Con-
nell, who is now a saint in glory, tell about the
murderin villains before I left swate Ireland."

This conversation continued some time, and
even after they retired to bed they talked about
the poor slaves. They all went to sleep with
the expectation that their mother would renew
her account of these unfortunate people, which
she did at no distant period, as my little readers
will learn by the next chapter.

CHAPTER II.

THE next evening, the children having finish-
ed their tasks, and being left alone with their
mother and Biddy, their thoughts naturally
turned to the subject that had so deeply engross-
ed their attention the night before.

" Mother! " said Jenie, " Charlie says that
in this country there are slave men and slave
women; they don't make slaves of little children, do they, and burn *their* faces, and whip
them till the blood runs?"

"Yes, my daughter, the slaveholders make
slaves of just such little girls as you are. Sometimes they sell them away from their mothers
so they can never see them again. Then they
force the mothers to work very hard and leave
them no time to take care of their children; and
sometimes these children go nearly naked —
have scarcely anything to wear, and not enough
to eat."

" Why don't their mothers get them something?" said Jenie.

" All the money their fathers and mothers

get they are compelled to give their masters, so that they can get neither suitable food nor clothing, and they are obliged to leave their little boys and girls to take care of themselves, like the pigs; and I have heard it said that they are sometimes fed in a trough as the pigs are, and on food almost as coarse. I think this is not often done, however."

"If they will come here, I'll give them some of my bread and milk," said Phil, who stood leaning on his mother, his chin on her knee, and eyes and ears both wide open to catch every word that was said about the little slaves.

"These people," continued Mrs. Selden, "do almost all the work that is done in the States in which they live. They raise nearly all the cotton that is used in this country, and most of the rice, and make a great deal of the sugar. Yet they don't get enough of this cotton for their own use, nor of the rice or sugar either.

"The slaves sometimes wear what is called *negro cloth*, which is made of very poor, coarse wool, with some cotton perhaps, and I have seen the hair of cattle mixed in it. This makes a pretty warm dress, but we should think it very rough and ugly if we were obliged to wear it.

The women in some cases wear a dress of tow cloth made of a single piece, and sewed up like a bag, with a string in one end to draw it around the neck; and many are seen with a few rags only tied above the hips and hanging mid-way to the ancle.

"I do not wish, dear children, to represent slavery to you worse than it really is. Some slaves are well clothed and have a plenty to eat, but as a general thing, very little attention is paid to their comfort. You know horses are treated very differently here. Some are well cared for — always have fine blankets and plenty of oats, while others are half-starved and are very poor and spiritless. It is so with these people; some are treated better than others; but all are regarded as inferior beings, and kept only for the master's use."

"Do they make slaves of little babies?" asked Jenie, "such tiny little babies as Mrs. Walker's? Mother, I love Mrs. Walker's baby dearly — it is a *dear* little thing. They don't call such babies slaves, do they?"

"Yes, Jenie, the wicked men who make the laws in the States where the slaves are, have made one that says, all the children of slave

mothers shall be slaves for life. A great many
of the mothers work in the cotton fields and in
the rice swamps, and they bind their infants on
their backs and carry them in that way while
they are hoeing and planting. They use very
heavy hoes, and the labor is very hard. Sometimes they lay their infants down in a corner of
the fence, but generally they are afraid to do
this because of snakes and other reptiles. Very
often they are left in a cabin alone, or with
some old woman who is not capable of taking
care of them, and the poor little things cry very
hard and suffer very much."

"The babies can't work any for their masters," said Jenie, "and what do they want of
them?"

"That is very true," replied Mrs. Selden;
"they cannot work when they are small, but
when they grow to be large boys and girls, and
men and women, their services will be very
valuable. If the masters did not keep these
children till they were grown up, they would
have to buy those already grown, and that is
very expensive. Sometimes they think it cheaper
to buy infants and raise them. The other day
when your father sold some pigs to Mr. Miller,

you remember that he weighed them, and perhaps you know that he got four cents a pound.
In the same way, infants are sometimes weighed
and sold by the pound!   American slave-traders,
however, regard them as *rather* more valuable
than pigs."

"Saint Patrick keep us!" cried Biddy, who
catching up Phil and pressing him to her bosom
seemed seized with an apprehension that in
some way or other *he* might be taken away and
sold with the pigs.

"Saint Patrit keep us!" responded Phil,
whose attention was diverted by this new expression, with which he seemed right well
pleased.

"Its a purty land of liberty I've come to!"
resumed Biddy.   "Who would iver drame that
they sell babies here as they sell pigs!   Sure,
but the landlords are cruel in Ireland; they're
ready to take the last pratie a man has, but
they'd niver be thinkin of taking away the
darlint babe from the mother of it, at all at all."

Perhaps some of my little readers never saw
such a person as Biddy.   She was a warm-
hearted Irish girl, and like most of the Irish was
a Roman Catholic.   You have all heard the

expressions "God bless you!" "Heaven be merciful!" and the like. These are short prayers; and the Catholics in *their* prayers instead of always addressing God, sometimes address the mother of Jesus, and the Apostles, and others who were regarded as holy people that have lived in different ages of the world.

Charlie, who had been an attentive listener all this time, inquired if an abolitionist, then, was a person who was trying to get these people free, so that the mothers could take care of their children.

"Certainly," replied Mrs. Selden.

"Well, mother," said Charlie, "Ned Miller says *he* is no abolitionist. Should'nt you thing every body would be an abolitionist?"

"Every body ought to be, my child."

"I am one," said Jenie. "I don't want them to treat little girls in that way."

"And so am I," said Phil.

"And sure ye'd be a disgrace to the mother that bore ye, if ye were not," responded Biddy.

"Do they often sell children by the pound?" inquired Charlie, very thoughtfully.

"I think it is not a common practice, though it has been done in many instances," said the mother. It *is* very common, however, to sell children, and men and women too, as horses and cattle are sold. They are often put up at auction with mules and other animals, and sold to the highest bidder. Sometimes the man who buys the husband will not purchase the wife, although he implores him to do so with tears in his eyes. The husband is taken away, and sometimes placed in what is termed a coffle — a long row or gang of slaves all fastened together — and then they are driven through the streets as Cæsar drives the oxen. The husband and wife never see each other again. The driver carries a long whip, and pistols and bowie knife besides."

"What does he carry those for?" asked Charlie.

"These slaves," said the mother, "must necessarily be very unhappy and discontented, having been torn away from their friends and their homes. Not unfrequently do they prefer death to this situation. This renders them disobedient, for which the driver whips them; and if they refuse to submit or attempt to escape they are shot! The body of a slave thus killed is thrown aside and left to be buried by some chance hand, or to be devoured by dogs!"

"Sure, mistress," exclaimed Biddy, "if iver I heard the like of that! They shoot a man down like a dog in this country, because he loves liberty, and then lave him for the dogs to ate! Oh, shame on them!"

"Speaking of the separation of families," resumed Mrs. Selden, " reminds me of an incident I heard related not many days since.

"A slaveholder owned a woman who had two fine children, one of which he sold. At this the mother mourned exceedingly — she wept loud and long, for which the master ordered her to be flogged. Soon after, the remaining child was sold ; this made the mother distracted. She wept all day, and even in the night her dismal wailing filled the air. She ran up and down the streets — pulled out her hair, and tore up the very earth in her madness. Her constant cry was, ' Me have no children! Will no good massa pity me ? Wicked massa sell me child.' Then running up to the passers-by she would exclaim, ' Me go into massa's house, and into massa's yard, and into me hut, and me no see 'em!' Then shaking herself violently, she would say, ' Me heart go so, for wicked massa sell me children. Oh, dear! what shall me do ?' "

"Mother, would it make you crazy if they should sell me, and Phil, and Charlie away from you?" asked Jenie.

"Oh, my child! I dare not think of it. I fear I should bear it no better than the slave mother."

"But I won't be sold," cried Phil.

"Nor I neither," responded Jenie.

"That ye shan't," said Biddy, "and evil would come upon them that would take the like of ye."

THE SLAVE BABY'S COMPLAINT.

Oh mother! dear mother! why leave me alone
   From the dawn of the morning till night?
Your poor little girl is so sad when you're gone
   And she suffers with hunger and fright.

There's no one comes near me when sick and in pain
   But a woman that's crabbed and old,
And though she's so deaf she can't hear me complain,
   She does nothing but punish and scold.

The baby at master's is bigger than I
   And could wait on itself if they'd let it;
They go to it quick if it happens to cry,
   And there's nothing it wants, but they get it.

Then what is the reason they drive *you* away,
   When I want you should always be here
To feed me when hungry and help me to play,
   And to call me your own little dear?

B. S. J.

CHAPTER III.

ONE day Mr. and Mrs. Selden were sitting in the parlor discussing the propriety of telling children of the suffering and wrong that exist in the world — of the inhumanity that man practices towards his fellow man.

It was rarely that Mr. Selden and his wife differed in regard to the management of their children ; but in this matter of telling them about the slaves, they did not altogether agree. He could not bear the thought that the joyousness of their young spirits should be checked by the contemplation of such terrible cruelties. Coming home one day, he had found Jenie engaged in examining very intently a picture of a slave tied to a post and being whipped very cruelly, with this inscription :

"Oh, don't, massa ! Don't !"

He leaned over her, and as she tossed the golden ringlets from her eyes, he saw they were filled with tears. She threw her little arms around his neck as he took her to his embrace. Neither father nor child spoke, but the gentle heavings of her bosom made him fear that at too early an age she was becoming acquainted with the history of crime.

Mrs. Selden reminded her husband that their children would be learning these sad stories from one and another, and it was best for parents to instruct them in regard to slavery and other evils, that a proper impression might be made --that they might have a just abhorance of wrong, and enlightened views of the course to be pursued toward the wrong-doer.

"And besides," said she, "benevolent enterprises have received great advantage from the moral influence of children. Nobody hesitates to instruct them in temperance principles, or to portray the evils of their violation; and many a poor drunkard has been raised from the gutter, and baptised into newness of life, through the saving power of his little child! How many a poor mother, reduced to want and starvation, has had reason to bless the influence of her young boy! They are effective preachers of righteousness; and their freedom from guile, and clearness of vision, render them powerful agents for good when properly instructed."

At this moment Charlie entered the room, and

with a countenance all animation and delight
said : —

"Father! did you know that Mr. Wright gave
me this book the other day? It is called "A
KISS FOR A BLOW," and it shows how we ought
never to injure those who injure us, but that we
should always return good for evil. I've been
reading this morning how he visited the schools
and asylums in Boston and Philadelphia, and
always taught the children to be very kind and
obliging to each other. Then he plays with them
a great deal. In one place he tells of a royal old
Elm that stands on Boston Common under which
children have played for two hundred years.
There, he says, he often assembles with fifty
or a hundred, and they frolic, and laugh, and
have glorious times. He plays tag, and ball
and battledore, and runs races with them ; and
sometimes they all take hold of hands and form
a great long row and march across the Common.
It must look queer. How I wish I could be with
Mr. Wright and those children under that royal
old Elm. Father! when you go to Boston
again, I hope you'll take me. He tells stories
too. I've been reading of one he told them
about two boys who pretended they had been

fighting in love ; and as I read how they stood before their father with black eyes and bloody noses, and told him they had been fighting because they loved each other, I laughed outright. People don't fight when they love each other, and so the children said — they thought the boys told a falsehood. I guess the boys and girls he talked with, that seemed so good and kind, and understood peace principles so well, are all abolitionists — don't you, mother ? "

" I hope they are," replied Mrs. Selden. Mr. Selden saw that the logic of his wife was altogether sound in reference to what she had been telling her children ; still he loved them so well, and was so desirous to make them happy, that he shrunk from the thought of having a single shadow fall on the sunlight of their young existence. But he saw that even if it were best, and he desired ever so much to keep the evils of the world from their view, it could not now be done. They were getting too old, and had become too deeply interested in what they had heard, not to desire to hear more. So he concluded that his wife might as well make thorough work of it, at least so far as Charlie was concerned, and tell him as much about the system of slavery as he was able to understand.

Mr. Selden went to his counting house, and the conversation between the mother and child was soon resumed. But they had not proceeded far before Charlie proposed to go for Phil and Jenie, thinking they would want to hear too.

"Never mind Phil," said the mother; "you may bring Jenie."

The little girl followed her brother into the parlor, and much to the surprise of the parent, brought in her hand a beautiful embroidered apron. It had been purchased for her but a few days before, and was an article she valued very highly. Looking up with the greatest earnestness she said —

"Mother! will you send this to the little slave girl?"

Mrs. Selden was deeply moved by this instance of generosity and pity on the part of her little daughter, and in her heart she prayed God she might ever be thus, so that in after life her self-sacrificing and compassionate spirit might serve to bless and purify the world.

To make the child understand that the apron could not well be sent, and even if it could, would not be very useful, and that she had better take her pennies and buy tracts and send them

to the slaveholders, that they might be convinced
that slavery was wrong, was a work that required some time.

So fearful was the mother that she should not
sufficiently encourage the beautiful spirit of the
child, that she allowed her to sell the apron and
purchase an anti-slavery book, which she sent to
a distant relative residing at the south, and which
Jenie fondly hoped would show him that slavery
was wicked, and would induce him to give up all
the little boys and girls that he held.

" I've been thinking a great deal," said
Charlie," about the prisoners we saw the other
day. You said they were kept in prison as a
punishment for crime. I should think the slaves
did not fare much better, and I suppose they are
not criminals. You said they worked out doors
raising cotton, and rice, and making sugar; and
the prisoners I know have to work in their cells
and be shut up all the time, and that must be
very bad. Do they build such great houses for
the slaves to live in as that prison, and have such
little cells, and do they have their food cooked
for them as the prisoners do ? "

" No, dear. I wish they had food as good as
the prisoners have, and houses as comfortable as

their cells. Their huts or cabins are very rude and cheerless. Sometimes they are made of clay — generally of logs, and often in the far south, of stakes and the leaves of the palmetto. These huts are very open, frequently having neither door, nor floor, nor chimney. Only think how uncomfortable it must be to live on the cold, damp ground, and in a place so open that it would not protect you from the tempest. Some of these poor beings are sometimes driven from their rude dwellings by the pitiless storm, the rain coming in from every quarter till there is no dry place even for the sole of the foot. They seek shelter in the huts of others, but oh, how glad would they be to find so warm and dry a spot as the prisoner's cell!"

CHAPTER IV.

"As you have mentioned the convicts in the State's Prison," said Mrs. Selden to her son, " I would like to show you how much more regard is paid to *their* wants, than to those of the slaves. I have already told you of their miserable huts, and you know there can be none of the comforts of home in such a wretched place."

" When the rain comes in and drives them out," said Charlie, " don't their beds and everything get wet ?"

" They have nothing that can properly be called a bed, so many persons say, who have lived in the south, and are well acquainted with their situation. They are generally furnished with one old blanket, and sometimes two. Some have a bundle of straw or a few old rags to lie on, while others sleep on the cold ground. They would consider themselves fortunate indeed could they have such nice beds as the prisoners have.

"I do not wish you to think the situation of the prisoner by any means a pleasant one. Oh! it is dreadful to be shut out from the beautiful world, from all the sources of happiness, almost from the sunlight and the refreshing air of heaven; to be confined in a narrow cell, and never hear the sound of a human voice — as is the case of some prisoners — or be allowed to look upon a human face, save that of the grim keeper who controls the heavy bolt that confines the sufferers in that solitary abode. Oh! the very thought of it makes my blood run cold, and I wonder how human beings ever could have devised such a mode of torture. But when I think of the slave, I see that he is the victim of a system that far exceeds in cruelty any form of punishment ever invented."

"Do tell me how it is, mother; I cannot see," said Charlie, "how slavery can be worse than that."

"Criminals are generally imprisoned," she replied, "for a few years only — the period of the slaves' bondage in the great prison house of oppression ends but with death. The convict, when his term expires, goes out a *free* man. He can return to his home and his friends, if

he have any; he can choose his own employment, and pursue his own happiness as it pleases
him best.   If he has truly repented of his
crime, he will, in a great measure, be restored
to society, and can enjoy life as well as before.
The slave looks forward to no time when *he*
shall go out a free man.   If he has been separated from his wife and children, he indulges in
no pleasing expectation that in a few years or a
few months he may return to those he loved so
well.   There are prisoners who know, that although *they* are shut up in a gloomy cell, their
children are enjoying freedom, the care of
friends and the comforts of life.   The slave
feels that *his* children are smarting under the
lash, and that they have no kind friend to protect
them, and that they are doomed to the deepest
degradation and misery.   The prisoner is sus-
tained by the expectation of having his freedom
again — of being the master of himself.   The
slave pines under his affliction, his heart fails
him, his spirit is broken by the crushing power
of slavery, and he lies down in despair, feeling
that a night of endless bondage has closed in
upon the hopes, the happiness and the liberty
of himself and three millions of his race."

" Three millions ! mother ?" said the astonished boy. " Mr. Gardner told us yesterday there
were only about twenty millions of people in
the United States ; — are three millions of them
slaves ? "

" It is a mortifying thought, my child, yet it
is nevertheless true. When we were in Philadelphia last summer, you were astonished at
the multitude of people that were passing up
and down the streets and crowding the shops.
Had you gone from the Navy Yard to Ken-
sington, from the Delaware to the Schuylkill,
and counted all the inhabitants of that great
city, you would have had but a small part of
the number of slaves. Indeed there are more
than twelve times as many of these oppressed
and suffering people as you would have found
persons in that place. And I believe you
could hardly go to any one of these three
millions, and ask him if he would be willing to
exchange his situation for that of the convict,
endure for a few years confinement in a close
cell, and then forever after have his freedom,
but he would be rejoiced to make the exchange.
But let any man go to the convict, and tell him
that instead of remaining in the solitary cell a

few years, he can be made a slave for life, and then ask him if he would choose the latter: the convict would think him a madman for putting the question. "

" But, mother, you said some men were imprisoned for life. Would not such rather be slaves than live always in their cells ?"

"I cannot tell how a man would feel under such circumstances ; still, I believe even then he would much prefer the prison," said the mother." In the prison he is sure of comfortable food and clothing, and of not being greatly over-worked. In slavery he is liable to be starved, to go nearly naked, to be compelled to work sixteen or eighteen hours a day. Although a prisoner in close confinement, he is regarded as a man ; by the law, he is recognised as a human being ; by the people he is spoken of as a member of the human family. In slavery he is looked upon as a brute ; he becomes a piece of property ; he has an owner who may inflict untold wrongs upon him, and no voice will be raised in opposition. This consideration alone, my child, would induce every man who has any appreciation of his manhood, who has any sense of the dignity of his position as a member of the human race, to choose the convict's cell for life rather than the lot of the American slave!"

"Were I to choose, mistress, I'm sure *I'd* niver be a slave," said Biddy, who had entered the room and heard the foregoing conversation. She had brought with her Phil, her darling pet, whose attention was attracted from his play by the rising spirit of Biddy, which was manifested by her earnest tone. When *she* expressed an opinion, Phil always felt called upon to sustain her. Consequently he informed his mother that he never would be a slave either.

"And," said he, "if the naughty men should come here, Charlie, would'nt I shoot them with my bow and arrow?"

"Phil don't understand peace principles very well, does he, mother?" asked Charlie.

"No, my dear, he is a little boy and don't know much about any kind of principles. He must not talk of shooting people though, even with his bow and arrow."

"You asked me, Charlie, the other day, if food were cooked for the slaves. Generally it is not, though sometimes one of their number prepares it, but it is always coarse and poor. On many plantations, or farms, as you would

call them, they give each full grown slave a
peck of corn a week.   After working in the
hot sun all day, they go home at dark very sad
and very weary, thinking how their poor little
children have wanted them when they were
away; and instead of sitting down to rest and
finding a comfortable supper, they have to grind
or pound their corn, and bake their hoe-cake,
and 'tis often past midnight before this and their
other work is done."

"What is hoe-cake?" asked Jenie.

"It is bread made of corn meal and water,
and baked before the fire on an old hoe," said
the mother, "and quite well satisfied would
many of the slaves be with this if they could
only get enough of it.   It is the testimony of
many who have lived in the South, that 'thousands of slaves are pressed with the gnawings
of cruel hunger during their whole lives.'   Boats
on the Mississippi river, when stopping over
night, are often boarded by slaves begging for a
bone or a bit of bread to satisfy their hunger.
They always seem very thankful for these
favors, and often a poor crust will call forth a
strong expression of gratitude.

"In a conversation I lately had with a friend

who had seen much of slavery in his trading voyages on that river, he said, that on one occasion when he was stopping at a plantation landing, a bright little slave boy came on to his boat and begged for something to eat. He gave him some bread and butter. The poor child, delighted with the bountiful gift, looked at him, and with gratitude beaming from his face, said, in his own uneducated dialect, 'When I dies and goes to God, I'll tell him that you gib me dis.' Happy, my dear children, will it be for us all, if, when the poor slave goes into the presence of its Father-God, it shall tell of acts of kindness *we* have done !"

" But, mistress," saidBiddy, " the slave sure can't suffer from the hunger-pain as I've seen my own people do at home. Oh! but the like of that I hope niver to see again."

" But then," rejoined Charlie, " they are not hungry all their lives, as some of the slaves are."

" That's true for ye. I've seen many a man who had been well to do, and had always a bit and a sup to give the stranger, who was left without a morsel in his cabin, and, God help him! his children crying for bread, and the

darlint wife looking so sad and so sorrowful
like, and all bekase the crops failed them, and
the praties they did raise were not fit even for
the pig to ate. Sure, I've seen many a sight
there that made my heart sore, and at this
blessed minit I'm a fearing that hundreds
haven't a handful of male in their cabin.

"Ye've a kind heart, master Charles, and I
love ye for it, and if ye had seen what I did
before I left the ould country, 'twould be after
melting itself into tears. The poor little childer
were nothing but skin and bone, and went about
so silent and so strange like, that it hurt me
heart to look at them. They had done crying,
and had done asking for bread, for they knew
there was none. And oh, but it was hard on
the mothers, for the laugh of their darlints that
was like a song to them was gone! and they
knew that they all must die, and not have even
a friend perhaps to carry them to the church-
yard. And the fathers too, who had kept up
brave hearts as long as they could, when they
saw the dead eyes of them they loved, and saw
their beautiful boys and girls become so ghost-
like they hardly knew them, and they not able
to beg a bite for them, or get a stroke of work

to do themselves; God save them! but it was hard."

"Biddy!" said Charlie, whose eyes were swimming in tears, "wouldn't these people rather be slaves?"

"That I can't say," replied Biddy, "for when the head is distracted-like, it's hard saying what a man would do if only himself was concerned; but there's not one of them, that I saw, would have been willing to have had a childer made a slave to save *it* from starvation. Sure, but the curse of God would have followed them if they would. And as for meself, I'd rather starve a thousand times, if it be God's will, than to be made a slave by the will of man."

"Biddy is right," said Mrs. Selden, turning to her children; "it is far better to die of starvation than to live in slavery. Besides, if you are in slavery you are liable to die of want as many a poor slave has done. Then you would be as badly off as the Irish in that respect, and subject to a multitude of other evils to which they are strangers."

THE HUNGRY SLAVE BOY.

Oh, will not some massa take pity on me ?
   I often am hungry from morning till night,
A bit of good food do I scarce ever see,
   And many a day I get hardly a bite.

What harm can so little a slave boy have done,
   That so sad and so hungry I always must go ?
When master calls for me, I'm ready to run
   And do what he bids me as well as I know.

I wish I could get just as much bread and meat
   As the free little boys and and the girls that I see !
Oh, how good it would be to have plenty to eat,
   And how strange it would seem for a slave boy like me !

And mother, she tells me that if when I die,
   I have done as I ought, and have always been good,
I shall live where the folks are all free in the sky,
   And where every body has plenty of food.

B. S. J.

CHAPTER V.

" I was telling you, my son," said Mrs. Selden to Charlie, " that some of the slaves did not get their corn pounded, and baked and eaten till nearly midnight. You know when your father is obliged to be up late at night, he does not rise early the next morning; but I often get breakfast for him after the rest have eaten. The slaves cannot do so. No matter how late they are up at night, they must be up early in the morning also. On many plantations they are required to be ready to go into the field at break of day. At the sound of the driver's horn all must hasten to their unpaid toil.

" That driver's horn!" said Mrs. Selden; " many a sweet vision of peace and comfort is destroyed by its unwelcome sound. The old slave, who has numbered his seventy winters, is dreaming perhaps of liberty — of the realization of his fondest hopes. He thinks his master has given him his freedom; that he has a little patch of ground he can call his own; that his wife, who was torn from him long, long ago, has been restored to his bosom; and his children, who were sold, some to go in one direction and some in another, have all obtained their freedom and returned to him. Oh, how happy he feels in the free family group and by his own free hearthstone. I say, he is dreaming this, perhaps, and the sound of the driver's horn dispels the illusion and he awakes to find that he is yet a slave ! that no tidings have been received of those he loves, that no prospect of liberty awaits him till he falls into the grave ! "

" Oh, mother," said Charlie, " it seems to me that I can see the old man now rising from his poor bed and getting ready to go to his work."

" And if you could see him, my son, you would see one with a heavy heart. You would behold such an expression of despair as you never saw on the human face before."

" I was thinking," said Charlie, "that the slaves lived so badly and had so little to eat that they could not work. I know I could not work if I were treated so."

" I'm sure I *would* not," said Biddy. "I'd not lift a finger. Stalk still I'd stand, and they might do their own work for all of me."

" There are many slaves," rejoined Mrs. Selden, "who would like to say what Biddy does but they dare not.   There are many who would refuse to work, if by so doing they would not be great losers rather than gainers."

" Gainers or losers, I'd not work without enough to eat and with nothing but rags to wear. I'd die first ! "

" The slaves are generally accompanied by an overseer or driver," continued Mrs. Selden, " whose business it is to see that each performs his alloted task.   If one from sickness or inability lags behind, he is urged on by the cutting lash.   There is no way of escape — they must work or be beaten, perhaps to death.   If they turn either to the right or to the left, and refuse to pursue the beaten track, they do it at the peril of their lives.   Whipping is almost universal; indeed, a slave who has never been whipped is a wonder in the country all around.   These overseers are notorious for their inhumanity ; for their shameless disregard of the common decencies of life ; for their utter abandonment of all moral principle, and their entire destitution of every good and generous feeling.   Even the masters, as unkind and inhuman as they are, in their souls abhor the overseer.   Still he is a necessary appendage to the plantation ; for if they keep slaves, they must keep somebody to whip them."

" But, mother, it is not necessary to whip them," interposed Charlie.

" Yes, my dear, it is," replied Mrs. Selden. " It may not appear so at first thought, but when we consider that the slave has no motive for action, that he may work ever so hard and earn ever so much, yet neither he, nor his wife, nor his children will be any better off: he will have, no property, none of the comforts of life; he will gain no consideration in the eyes of the world, but will still be looked upon as a brute, unworthy a place among men; will still be obliged to endure poverty, perhaps actual starvation; we know that his heart must sicken within him and that he cannot work; consequently all that is got out of him must be obtained by the power of the lash. If slavery be right, my child, the whipping is right also, for the former cannot be maintained without the latter.

" I have spoken principally of the plantation slaves, or field hands, as they are sometimes called. Besides these, there are many house servants, including cooks, table-waiters, chamber maids, nurses, seamstresses, and body servants.

" No more regard is paid to the wants or the comfort of these, than to those of the field hands, though the differance in their situation may give them some advantages.   Many who are familiar with southern life have stated that these servants have neither beds, nor chairs, nor tables in their own apartments, indeed none of the conveniences of life so indispensable to home enjoyments.   While they are likely to get better food and clothing than the field slaves, on the other hand, instead of having one overseer to please, they have many.   They are at the mercy of master, mistress, children, and indeed the whole household, who are each and all liable to fall into fits of passion and inflict upon them the most terrible cruelties.   Not unfrequently does the mistress herself ply the bloody lash, and the abhorred paddle, and sometimes in the heat of her fury will she seize the poker, or tongs, or broom, and fall upon the poor wretched slave with all the ferocity of a tiger.

" I am sorry, my son, to state this dreadful fact about women, who are supposed to be more gentle and kind than men; but slavery renders all hearts hard and flinty that have anything to do with it; it transforms them into unfeeling tyrants, and makes them commit deeds we blush to think of.

" Mr. Calvin H. Tate, of Missouri, relates a case of cruelty that occured on a plantation adjoining his father's, who was also a slaveholder. A young woman had her back so unmercifully cut by the lash that the garment next her skin was stiff from the running of the sores. This, with other things, made her so sick that she was obliged to leave the field. As soon as she reached the house she fell upon the floor entirely exhausted. Her mistress asked her what the matter was, but she gave no answer. She asked again, but there was no reply. 'I'll see,' she said, ' if I can't make you speak.' So taking the tongs she heated them red hot and seized hold of her feet, and then her legs and body, and at last in a rage took hold of her throat. The poor girl faintly whispered, ' Oh! Misse, don't — I'm most dead;' and presently the suffering creature expired.

" Oh, mother! I never heard of anything so unfeeling,"said Charlie. " I did not know there were such women in the world. I hope there are not many who do such wicked things."

" Should a woman fly at me with the poker

or tongs, I guess it's the last time she'd do the like of it," said Bibby, and her eyes flashed fire as she spoke. " It's meself that 'd show every one of them, they'd better not be after trying to trate me in that way. Sure, but I'd give them as good as they brought, and may be a little bit better," and in her excitement she began to roll up her sleeves and display a great pair of brawny arms which seemed to bid the offender beware! " They're a burnin disgrace to their sex, so they are, and if they'd dare to lay the weight of their little finger on me, I'd warrant me they'd niver forget Biddy O'Flannagan !"

" I doubt not you would do as you say," observed Mrs. Selden, "but your course would not be christian, or prudent either, if you valued your own life. In some states, Georgia, for instance, if a slave strikes a white person, he must suffer such punishment, not extending to life or limb, as the court may see fit to prescribe ; and for the second offence — the second blow — *he must suffer* DEATH ! There would be no alternative in your case, Biddy ; you would soon lose your life, for I know by your spirit that you *would* fight."

" Well, mistress, and would'nt I be quite as well off to be killed by the law, as to be killed by a brute of a woman? It's a purty law though you've made in this *free* country," continued Biddy, in the most contemptuous tone, " to kill one bekase he wo'nt paceably submit to be beaten to death with a poker! A purty law surely, and its a purty country I've come to !"

" Mother, do tell me," said Charlie, "why these people don't run away. What do they stay with the slaveholders for ? Why don't they go and live in some other place ?"

" Charlie, why does Mr. Willet's horse stay with him ? You say he treats him very badly, he don't give him enough to eat, or take any care of him, makes him draw such heavy loads that you sometimes think the horse will be drawn in two ; and when he is tired, you say he beats him, and makes him work until he is ready to fall down. You remember he ran away last summer, and Mr. Willet went after him. Perhaps you heard that some man took up the horse and kept him till the owner came. The horse stays with his master because he can't help it, don't he ? He submits to the treatment of which you complain because he can do no better. All the men about the country have horses as well as Mr. Willet, and when their's escape, they want assistance to retake them; consequently they will render all the aid necessary to enable Mr. Willet to keep *his* horse. It is just so with the slaves. The most of them remain where they are because they can't help it — because they can do no better. Their rights as human beings are utterly denied them, and the right of the master to hold them for his own use as horses are held, fully acknowledged by the community in which they live, by the law and the public sentiment of the entire South. Every man's hand is against them; every face they meet is the face of a foe. All the people around them have conspired together to keep them in bondage. They feel that the curse of slavery has pierced them to the soul; despair has settled down upon them; they are in the power of an oppressor from whom there is no escape; and like the prisoner in the Iron Shroud, of whom you were reading yesterday, they see the cold, heavy walls of slavery gradually closing in upon them, and they know they must finally be crushed to death beneath their ponderous weight."

CHAPTER VI.

Mrs. Selden generally allowed several days to intervene between their conversations on the subject of slavery. She wished to make a lasting impression upon the minds of her children, and she thought this could be done better by giving them a few facts only at a time. When the subject was resumed again, she said,—

" Charlie, perhaps I should have told you the other day, that many slaves have attempted, and succeeded too, in escaping from their masters. I was speaking then of the mass, of the great majority, who see no way of escape. It is not uncommon among the more daring spirits to watch for a favorable opportunity, and in the silence and darkness of midnight steal away and secrete themselves in a neighboring swamp, or make a bold push for a land of freedom. Their absence is quickly noted, and arrangements make for speedy pursuit. It is not unusual for several planters to join in a Slave Hunt — as such an expedition is called — and this Slave Hunt is one of the most brutal features of the system. The party are always well armed, for

they expect the slaves to make resistance, and
they prepare themselves to shoot them down if
they refuse to surrender. They are generally
accompanied by bloodhounds that have been
trained to the service of tracking fugitives, and
very often they lead the party directly to the
place where the poor slaves have taken refuge,
or follow on until they overtake them in their
flight.

"Perhaps these poor victims of oppression
are pressing onward, and onward, and their fear
of pursuit begins to subside; when lo! they
hear the deep baying of the hounds in the distance, and as the sound draws nearer, and
nearer, they hear mingled with it the yells and
execrations of the pursuers. Alas! what can
the poor fugitives do? They make one des-
perate struggle to escape — one frenzied rush
for life and liberty! They plunge into the
dense forest; they seek the most intricate way;
they strain every nerve, and summon all the
energies of their wearied nature for this last
effort. But it is all unavailing. The hounds
are upon them! The masters demand a surrender.

"The slaves spurn the command with all the

indignation of outraged men, and still attempt
to pursue their way. They are fired upon, at
first for the purpose of disabling them, and
although many a shot is lodged in their limbs
and shoulders, and their flesh is torn and man-
gled by the savage dogs, yet in the madness of
their despair they rush on, and on! At length
one or two are brought to the ground by the
deadly rifle. The fatal work is done! the rest
give up.

"The hunters glory in the triumph and exult
over the conquest of a few striken and famishing
men and women who desire to be free. They
mutter a few curses over the dead bodies of the
fallen, and as they gaze upon the yet warm and
quivering flesh of their victims, and see to what
fearful length the love of liberty carried them,
apparently no feeling of remorse is awakened
in their bosoms, no regret that such is the unhappy condition of a fellow man. They talk
only of the loss of property, then bind fast their
captives and prepare to return.

"The punishments inflicted upon these run-
aways," continued Mrs. Selden, "are almost
incredible. They receive sometimes one, two,
three, and even five hundred lashes on the bare

4

back — it's a strong man, though, who can take the latter and live. Sometimes they are compelled to wear heavy iron collars on their necks till the very flesh is worn from the bones; sometimes a chain with a heavy iron ball attached to it is fastened to the ancle, and the poor creature is obliged to drag that about day after day. Sometimes the victim is placed in the stocks — a machine which confines the feet and legs in an immovable position — and nearly starved to death; and sometimes one ear is cut off, and sometime several teeth are knocked out; and very often they are sold to the far South from whence they can never hope to escape. No offence is punished so severely as running away. Love of liberty appears to be regarded as the highest of crimes."

Biddy, Jenie and Phil were all present, and had been listening with the deepest attention. At length the former exclaimed, —

" Holy Mother save us! if what ye've been telling be true. Sure, mistress, I'd not belave it, had not your own lips been speaking it. I've seen many a fight in me own country at a Wake or a Fair, and the Orange boys and Ribbon men were cruel to each other; but then it's fighting for their religion they were, and that ye know, mistress, often makes a man savage like. But Slave Hunts! Saints preserve us! May the like niver disgrace swate Erin. Ye've men and women in this country then that are free to be hunted with guns and bloodhounds as wild bastes of prey are hunted. Sure, it's better to be free to die of famine in Ireland, than to have the freedom of a nager slave in Ameriky."

"Mother," said Jenie, "what do the women do with their children when they run away?"

"Many of them have none," replied the parent, "and those that have, sometimes take them also. Sometimes their children have been previously sold; and sometimes they leave them behind, expecting that in some way or other they can be got away afterwards."

"Well, mother," said Jenie, "you wouldn't run away and leave Phil and me with the cruel men, would you?"

"No dear, I should rather stay. The thought that my little children were slaves, would make me very wretched, and destroy all the pleasure of being free myself. Many slave mothers feel in the same way; so long as their children must be slaves they choose to remain slaves also."

" Well," said Phil, who was always seeking ways to punish the tyrant, " I should think the slaves would set the dogs on the masters. *I* would, and make them tear the ugly men all to pieces."

" I'm sure it ought to be done, master Phil," responded Biddy, " and if the dogs were but sensible-like they'd be after doing it."

" That would be returning evil for evil," said Jenie, " would it not ? Mother says that is wrong."

" But the dogs would'nt bite their masters," observed Charlie. " Nobody could make old Tig do us any harm, and I suppose its just the same with their dogs. Mother, you said some time ago that some slaves did get away. Do tell us more about *them* ?"

" I will; you can hardly imagine though, my child, what difficulties lie in the way of the fugitive. If the slave is valuable and is not found immediately, handbills are circulated in every direction offering a reward of twenty, fifty, and sometimes two hundred dollars for his apprehension. There are men all around the country who would be glad to obtain this reward by seizing and returning him, so he is obliged to keep out of the sight of men, and travel only in the fields and woods, and hide himself in swamps, and dens, and caves. Often for weeks and months the haunt of the wild beast and the poisonous reptile is his only home; yet he had rather risk his life with these than to endure the cruelties of man. He fears less the beast of prey than the power of the oppressor. He lives on nuts, and fruits, and roots, and whatever he can pick up. After long, and lonely, and wearisome travel he succeeds in reaching a land of freedom."

"The slaveholders must be very different from other people, mother?" said Charlie, enquiringly. "I am sure no one that I know would be guilty of doing so wickedly. No one would set a dog upon a poor wretched woman who wanted to be free; no one would whip her for crying because her children were sold."

"Slaveholders are not so different from other people as you might at first suppose," observed Mrs. Selden. "I presume you are not acquainted with any who would *now* in his present situation do such cruel acts as I have been telling you about. But take a person and surround him for awhile with the hardening influ-

ences of slavery — let him daily witness extreme
sufferings and torture; give him power — let him
hold slaves, and feel that it is for his interest to
get a great amount of labor out of them; and
he would whip, and beat, and brand, and hunt
with dogs his wretched victims just as other
slaveholders do.

" The exercise of power over a fellow man
corrupts the human heart and turns it into a
heart of stone. When you become better acquainted with the world, my son, you will find
that many who are noted for cruelty, were once
kind and compassionate as any of the people
about you. The commencement of the reign
of some of the Roman Emperors was marked
by the greatest lenity and kindness; but so cor-
rupting was irresponsible power — power that
none dare attempt to restrain — that at length
they seemed to take pleasure in deluging Rome
with human blood! Thousands of human beings
were sometimes sacrificed in a single hour!

" I greatly desire to impress upon you, my
dear boy, the importance of cherishing and cul-
tivating all the good and generous feelings that
you have; and of suppressing all selfish and
revengeful thoughts. If you feel prompted to

speak a kind word to the unfortunate, to lend a helping hand to one in distress, to confer a favor upon the needy, always act out these feelings, and never suffer yourself to be restrained by a laugh or a sneer from your companions, or by the opposite course of those around you."

" Well, mother, I hope I shall always be a good boy, and I will *try* to act out my good feelings. The other day, Frank Hulton, whose mother has been sick all summer, and who is very poor and never buys anything for her children to play with, wanted my little cart — he said I had a wagon and did not need it. I felt like giving it to him, and almost said he might have it, but a selfish feeling came up that made me change my mind. I think now I will give it to him."

" Yes, dear, I hope you will not let the day pass without making glad the heart of Frank Hulton by the gift he desires.

THE FUGITIVE.

The night was cold and stormy
  When a dark browed man came forth,
And with quick and eager footstep
  Pressed onward to the north.

The lash that day was buried
  Deep in his quivering flesh,
And the crimson drops came trickling
  From wounds that bled afresh.

What seeks he in the shadow
  Of the deep and tangled wood?
Why lurks he in the forest
  Where wild beasts seek their food?

Why cringes he with terror,
  Why trembles he with fear
At every sound that falleth
  On his quick and listening ear?

Why does the blood-hounds baying
  That cometh to him now,
His dark cheek blanch with terror
  And with cold sweat bathe his brow?

Why rushes he so madly
  And with fleetest foot away,
As though no human barrier
  His onward course could stay?

He is fleeing from oppression —
From slavery's deadly ban;
He is seeking for the Freedom
His Creator gave to man.

God speed him in his efforts !
May he never be the prey
Of blood-hounds, or of tyrants
More merciless than they !

B. S. J.

CHAPTER VII.

CHARLIE was a great talker. He had an inquiring mind, and was always seeking the why and wherefore of every thing. Like other boys he often asked his mother to tell him stories, and unlike most boys he never wanted to hear any that were made up. He liked true stories — he asked for facts, for real events — he wanted to know about people and things. He was interested in her slave stories because she assured him that all her statements were literally true. Many a time he wished that these were made up stories, and that there were no slaves in the world.

Charlie talked a great deal with his father, and I think some of my young friends would like to know what their conversations were about; but in this little book I shall tell them only what his mother said about slavery.

Mr. Selden was always instructing his children, and when he went to town on business, or round the neighborhood in which he lived, he often took Charlie and went with him into all the shops and factories where the people work

on wood, iron, tin, brass, stone, clay, cotton,
wool, &c., and explained to him every thing
connected with their several handicrafts. He
frequently asked his father questions about the
slaves; but Mr. Selden did not say much to
him on this subject, so he generally preferred
talking with his mother.

He came home from school one day, evidently
somewhat perplexed. He immediately went to
his mother that he might tell her what Ned
Miller, one of his school-mates, had said about
the abolitionists. Charlie had been contending
that every one ought to be opposed to slavery,
and Ned, on the other hand said, "He didn't
care for the old niggers, and whipping was just
good enough for them." Charlie said, "We
talked about this at recess, and after we went
into school, as we sit on the same seat, we continued to talk. At last Mr. Gardner came along
and asked us what we were talking about. I
told him we were talking about the slaves. He
frowned and looked very much displeased; then
he said, 'Let me hear no more of that; you'd
better be talking about things that concern you
—you have no business with *them*.' Mother, I
never saw Mr. Gardner look so before. I am
sure this *is* a subject that concerns us."

" I was telling you not long since," rejoined
Mrs. Selden, " that many people about here are
not very different from slaveholders.   They
know that three millions of their fellow-citizens
are wearing chains — that they are enduring a
worse form of oppression than ever disgraced any
barberous age or nation ; yet they raise no voice
against it — they utter no protest — but allow the
slaveholder to go on and commit his crimes with
impunity, and not only that, but strengthen his
arm in the performance."

" Why, mother ! it seems to me that's the worst
part of the story," added Charlie.

" Yes," said Mrs.Selden, " what I have to tell
you of the indifferance of the people of the North
to this subject ; of their hostility to every movement for the overthrow of slavery ; and of their
actual support and sanction of the system, will
astonish you more, perhaps, than all I have told
you of the woes and sufferings of those in bonds.

" It seems almost impossible," continued the
parent, " to awaken anything like a determined
opposition to slavery except on the part of a
few ; but a strong feeling is daily shown in favor
of it, and a determination to maintain it, let the
sacrifice be what it may."

" But, mother, the people who live in the Northern States don't want men and women to be robbed of their wages, and compelled to live on corn as the pigs do, and live in such mean huts, and have their children sold away !" urged the enquiring boy.

" They *say* they don't, my child, yet their whole influence is in favor of slavery — both by *word* and by *deed* do they encourage the slave-holder to continue his wicked course."

" Why! don't they think it very wrong," asked Charlie, " to hunt men with dogs and shoot them down because they don't want to be slaves ? Perhaps though it's necessary, as you said the other day if men kept slaves they must keep somebody to whip them, or do it themselves, as they could not be made to work without. Are all the cruelties you have mentioned necessary to keep them on the plantations ? "

" Slaves are sometimes punished, doubtless, to gratify the rage of a master," said Mrs. Selden, " and to make them *feel* they are in the power of one they must not disobey ; still I think a great amount of cruelty is actually necessary in order to bring down the spirit of a man and make him grovel in the dust like a base reptile at the feet of a master. Man was never made for that condition ; he has within him a proud spirit that naturally spurns the restraints imposed upon him. Implanted in his bosom is a love of freedom ; it is part of his very being ; he has a desire to advance — to rise higher and higher ; and it takes strong cords and prisons, heavy bolts and bars, much scourging and beating, to break his spirit and confine it in the narrow dungeon of slavery.

" There is not an animal in creation that loves not its liberty, and it is only in strong iron cages that some can be confined ; it is only by great watchfulness, and long training, and much force that our horses and oxen even can be made to endure the bit and the yoke; and just in proportion as a man is more intelligent, more noble and exalted in his nature than the animals around him, in that same proportion must the power of those who claim dominion be increased to keep him in bondage.

" Yes, my child, much power and cruelty too are necessary to make and keep a man a slave. The foot of the oppressor must be on his neck *continually*, or he'll be up and away !

" And here let me observe that it is not the cruelties so much, that the abolitionists complain

of and wish to abolish, as the principle of holding
men in slavery — it is treating men as property
against which they protest. Most men claim
the right to do what they please with their
property, therefore it is not right to buy and sell
men and women and call them property, and
then they will not be subject to this abuse."

"I see now how it is," said Charlie; "if these
people were not slaves they would not be treated
so badly, so we should try to make them free,
and not expect they will be much better off while
they remain where they are."

"Yes, my dear, you understood me aright,"
replied Mrs. Selden.

"Mother, at one time when you were talking,
you said the slaves that ran away, sometimes
got to a land of freedom. I suppose you meant
they were free when they came into the Northern States. This is the land of freedom you
spoke of, is it not?"

"No, my son, there is no freedom *here* for
the slave. Would to heaven there was! If old
Tig should run away, though he might go ever so
far, even to Georgia, he would be your dog still,
would he not? and you could go and bring him
back."

"Yes, I understand that."

" Well," said the mother, " it is just so with
the master and the slave. The former can get
the latter if he can find him, and bring him back
from any part of the United States where he
may take refuge."

" Why, mother, is there no spot where the
slave would be free? That's bad enough! Why
what a dreadful condition he is in ! A slave
everywhere ! Suppose he should come and
live with us, would'nt he be free then ?"

" No, even at our own fireside he would still
be a slave — the master would claim him as *his*
property, and bring him back again if he could."

" Do tell," said Charlie, somewhat impatient-
ly, " where this land of freedom is ! I suppose
it's somewhere on the earth."

" Yes, there are many places where he would
be free. Canada is the place I referred to ; that
is where fugitives generally go."

" I know where it is, right north of us ; but
what makes them free when they get there ? "
asked Charlie.

" Canada is under the government of Great
Britian, and that has declared that one man
shall not hold another man as property and
compel him to work as he does his cattle without

pay. The slaveholder might go there and demand the fugitive, but the English government
would scout his claim to his fellow man, and
laugh him in the face ; and at the same time
would declare the poor slave free, and make him
as safe as any of its own citizens."

" Do many slaves go there, mother ? "

" It is said some twenty thousand have settled
there within a few years past."

" Well," said the boy, who had a very reten-
tive memory, and could call up all he ever
heard as occasion demanded, " I remember that
Mr. Gardner told us once that the government
of the United States was the best government in
the world. I should think the government of
Canada was better, as it does not let one man
hold another man in bondage."

" So far as slavery is concerned, it is far better," replied the parent ; " still I do not suppose
Mr. Gardner meant to tell you an untruth. No
people have ever laid down such broad principles of freedom and equality as we have, and
none have ever so shamefully trampled these
principles in the dust."

" But he told us," returned Charlie, " that the
English government was *very* oppressive."

5

" And so it is," added the mother." "You
have heard Biddy talk of the poverty of the
Irish — their extreme destitution is owing most-
ly to the oppressive acts of the British government. And when you go to England you will
find a state of things but little better. In the
cities you will see the most costly edifices in the
neighborhood of the most miserable hovels ; the
titled nobleman rolls through the streets in his
luxurious coach, while the beggar searches for
kitchen offals in the filthiest of gutters ! In the
country, too, you find the same extreme of poverty and wealth ; — on the one hand stands the
lordly mansion, with beautiful gardens, extensive
parks and magnificent forests, while all around
it, men are crushed and degraded, compelled to
incessant toil, and in their extreme destitution
craving the very food upon which the hounds of
the nobility are fed ! Americans sometimes go
there and talk against this inequality and oppression, but they are always met with the indignant reply, 'We don't hold SLAVES, as *you*
do.'

" One of our good abolitionists, who was in
England a year or two since, was deeply moved
by the extreme destitution and suffering of the

poorer classes — it made his heart ache to witness the oppression there.

"One day he obtained permission of the keeper of Her Majesty's jewels to examine the crown of the young queen, which is worth three millions of pounds sterling. Having learned its immense value, his mind reverted to the fact that thousands of the poor and needy had been robbed in order to sustain the monarch with her royal insignia, and feeling too that a great amount of suffering might be alleviated by applying the wealth thus lying useless to feed those who were starving at the gates of her palace, he involuntarily exclaimed, 'Thank God, I don't live in a country where one woman wears jewels worth millions of pounds, while others are dying for want of food!' A gentleman present hearing his remark, sarcastically replied, 'Thank God, I don't live in a country that holds SLAVES!' And 'tis ever thus. When an American abroad speaks of the oppression he sees around him, he is tauntingly told,

'Go, loose your fettered slaves *at home*!'"

"Well, mother," said Charlie, "if I understand you, the English government will not give up slaves to their masters, because the people do not make slaves of each other; and they will not acknowledge that one man has a right to another man. Now the people here in the North do not make slaves of each other, and I suppose if one of our neighbors, Mr. Parker for instance, should try to make slaves of any of us, the people would deny that he had a right to do so."

" They certainly would," returned Mrs. Selden.

" Why then," enquired Charlie, " do they give up the southern slaves, if they do not acknowledge that a man here has a right to make slaves of his neighbors ?"

" They surrender them," said the parent, "because they have agreed to do so, or they do it voluntarily because they wish to keep them in bondage."

" How have they agreed to ? Do tell me something about that."

" I will, my child; but in order to do it, I must go somewhat into the nature of our government, which I cannot do at this time. When a convenient opportunity offers, I will tell you as much about it as I think you can understand."

CHAPTER VIII.

" You have learned from your school books,"
said Mrs. Selden to her son, " that the United
States were once colonies of Great Britain."

" Yes," interposed Charlie, " I know all about
that. George the 3rd taxed their tea, and glass,
and paper very unjustly, and slighted their peti-
tions, and kept soldiers here that burnt some of
their towns and killed the people. The colonists
refused to submit to this, and declared themselves independent; but they had to fight a seven
years' war before they got their independence."

" I see you have learned the story," remarked
the mother smilingly. " I wish the injustice of
America as well as that of England had been
taught you also. Have you learned, my child,
that when the colonists separated themselves from
the mother country, they issued a Declaration of
sentiment in which they said, God gave to all
men, that is to every man, a right to liberty?"

"No, I don't know much about that, but if
they said all men had a right to liberty, I suppose the people of the present time think they
were greatly mistaken, as they take away the

liberty of three millions, and hunt them with dogs and guns if they attempt to obtain it. The people who wrote that must be a great deal better than the people who live now. But, mother, I don't understand this matter. You say when we became an independent nation the people declared that all were free; how did we happen to have slaves in this country then?"

"Alas! my child, that Declaration did not make all men free. We had slaves here at that time; and the very men who said to all the world, every man has a right to liberty, and appealed to the Supreme Judge of the Universe to witness their sincerity, at the same time held their fellow men in slavery! Their own plantations were watered with the sweat and tears of suffering bondmen!"

"Why, how strange that was!" cried Charlie. "Didn't they *mean* what they said?"

"I cannot tell what they meant," added Mrs. Selden, "only as I see their conduct. We must judge them as we do other people. If a man should declare that all men had a right to their own property, and it ought not to be taken from them, and yet should steal it as often as he could get a chance, we should begin to suspect that he was not altogether sincere in his professions; or that he spoke only abstract truth without any design of making a practical application."

"I suppose," said Charlie, "that none of the men that I know anything about held slaves. I've read about many of the brave generals in the war, and they seemed to be very good and sincere. General Washington was a great man, wasn't he, mother? Although you have told me many times that war was wrong — that we ought always to carry out peace principles and forgive our enemies; yet I never could help feeling that I should like to be a brave general like Washington, and have such a gay horse, and fine uniform, and a sword by my side, and a feather in my cap. Mother, I should be *very* great and *very* grand! Wouldn't you be proud of me? I don't know but this is wicked, but I *should* like to be a great general."

"Would you not rather save life than destroy it? Would you not rather be a good man, my child, one whom the poor and needy would remember with gratitude? one who has the satisfaction of feeling that he has delivered the poor stricken slave from the hand of the spoiler? He only is truly great who is a good man. Strive *earnestly* then to.be good, if you would be great."

" But, mother, you won't let me strive in the right way. I was just telling you I would like to be a general, and if I could be such a general as Washington, I should be both great and good. Every body says *he* was a good man."

"Washington," replied the mother, " doubtless had good traits of character, but he was a *warrior*, and a SLAVEHOLDER, and to be either is inconsistent with christian principles."

" A slaveholder !" cried the astonished boy. " *General Washington a slaveholder!* Why, mother, was he so cruel as to take little children from their mothers, and compel men to work for him without pay ?"

" The latter he certainly did, and it is generally reported that he was. guilty of the former. Let that be as it may, it is enough to know that he was a slaveholder. I ask not whether these slaves are well or ill treated ; indeed I know that no one can be well treated while a slave. The very act of depriving a man of his freedom is an act of unmitigated cruelty."

" Do you know certainly," inquired Charlie, " that he was a slaveholder ? I have always heard every body speak well of him, and wherever I have read anything about him it has always been in his praise. Mr. Gardner told us once, too, that the name of Washington would ever be beloved by every true American. I should not think his slaves would love it much. Perhaps Mr. Gardner thinks they are not true Americans. Why do the people call him good if he was a a slaveholder? Slaveholders are not good, are they?"

"People have different ideas of goodness. Some think that those who take their neighbor's service without wages and give them naught for their work; who shut out the light of knowledge, and the truths of the Gospel from the human mind; who darken the intellect, break the spirit, beat and brand the bodies of their fellow men, are true christians. And some think that those who go to war and slay their brethren, and trample out their life's blood on the red field of battle as you talk of doing, are good men."

"Oh, no! mother, you misunderstood me. I never wanted to kill any body. I should think I was a very wicked boy if I wanted to do that. I only thought I'd like to be a great general."

"What makes a great general, Charlie? It

is laying and executing great plans for the overthrow and destruction of those whom God has
told you to forgive and love as brethren.   It is
skill in the work of human butchery !"

"Well, if that makes a great general, I'll never
wish to be one again," rejoined Charlie.   " I
was'nt thinking of the dead and the dying: I
was thinking only of the grand music that I've
heard at trainings, and the prancing horses, and
the plumes, and the swords, and handsome dress,
and all that.   But I know trainings are wrong as
well as war.   I've read about them in the book
Mr. Wright gave me, and so I won't wish to be
a trainer even.   I think you ought to have let
me gone to hear Mr. Wright when he was here ;
I am afraid I shall never have another chance."

" I hope you will.   I would much rather, my
son, that you would take a peace man and an
abolitionist for your model, than a great general
and slaveholder.   The influence of the former
blesses the world, softens the hearts of men and
makes them speak · words of love, and tenderness — it carries hope and rejoicing to the bosom
of the pining, down-trodden slave ; while the
influence of the latter awakens hatred and the
spirit of resistance — it tramples into the dust

the hopes and the rights of our equal brethren.

"But we have wandered very far from the subject we began to talk about, which was, the agreement the States made with each other to give up fugitive slaves."

"Yes, mother, I want to hear about that. Last evening, when Mr. Hastings was here, he and father were talking about the government, or Constitution, or something I don't know what, being anti-slavery and pro-slavery. I didn't understand them. Can you explain it to me?"

"I will try," returned the parent. "All the states, with the exception of Massachusetts, held slaves at the time the government was formed."

"What! the Northern States?" interrupted Charlie. "I never knew that they held slaves."

"Yes, they did, and I think we may reasonably infer that a slaveholding people would not form a constitution of government opposed to slavery, if they wished to maintain the system; and it certainly is doing them no injustice to suppose they wished to perpetuate it, inasmuch as they did not do it away."

"But, mother, I don't know as I understand what the constitution is. I've often heard father speak of it, and I thought it was some kind of a law every body ought to obey."

" Well, it is — we must obey it or suffer for our disobedience. When the colonies were contending against Great Britain, they thought it very desirable to be united ; so they formed a kind of league which served as a government, and their agreement was known as ' The Articles of Confederation.'   After peace was made, some of the colonies, or states, as they were then called, wished a stronger bond of Union, something that should fully protect the interest of all and unite them more closely together.   After much consultation they adopted in 1789 another form of government called the Constitution of the United States.   Each State has its own laws, and Governor and other officers ; but the Constitution is above them all, being the highest law in the land.   What *it* requires is superior to all other legal obligations."

" What does it say about the slaves ?" asked Charlie.

" It describes a class of persons like the slaves, and makes provision in regard to them, saying they shall be given up to the claimant, &c.   It matters very little, however, about the way it reads ; the people have always understood it to be in favor of slavery.   Both States and indi-

viduals have always surrendered fugitives under
it.   Though some have acknowledged that it
was a sin and a shame to do so, yet they said
the law required it."

"How did the slaveholders get back their
runaway slaves before they had a constitution?"
inquired Charlie. "Didn't the articles of confederation say that the masters might take them
wherever they could find them?"

"No, my child. If a State chose to give
them up, it did so, but there was no compulsion
in the case — no Constitution to require it — no
general understanding to demand it; and the
fact that they were not more frequently given
up, was a cause of sore complaint on the part
of the slaveholder.   Since 1789, the slave-
catcher has felt that he had a legal right to hunt
out his fugitives and drag them back from any
part of the Union where they had taken shelter;
and the people do not question his right to do it,
and very many stand ready to help him.

"And the men all around us, Charlie," continued Mrs. Selden, "our very neighbors and
friends, join with the slaveholders in sustaining
this wicked Constitution and all the laws that
are made under it, even those which justify the

master in all the terrible cruelties I have mentioned. They sustain a government under which
the poor mother is robbed of all her little ones,
and left with nothing to love, nothing to hope
for. Her very existence becomes a burden and
she longs to die! They sustain a government
under which man is robbed of all the joys and
hopes and objects of life; robbed even of the
right to the heart that beats in his bosom and the
immortal soul that God gave him!

"The free men of the north sit down to
make laws with those who rifle their neighbors'
pockets and steal away all their living; and not
content with that, rob them of their wives and
daughters, whom they subject to outrages of the
most brutal character.

"Slavery, my child, is the highest kind of
crime! It is a far greater sin than was ever
committed by any of the criminals that you
have seen. *They* were guilty of petty thefts
and robberies, and now and then one in the heat
of excitement had given a blow that destroyed
his fellow. These were all wrong, but slavery
is a system that embodies all these crimes on a
most stupendous scale. It robs millions of *every
thing*, and annually murders its thousands!

Yet the men who do these things are regarded as men fit to make laws for an enlightened and *christian* nation."

"Well, I'm sure," said Charlie, "that father has nothing to do with such a government."

"No, I hope not," replied the mother. "I trust he will never enter into a government with the oppressors of his race ; and that he will give no voluntary support to laws that deny equal liberty to all. I am glad, my son, that you are spared the deep mortification that I once saw a little girl experience."

"Tell me about it, mother."

"One evening at the house of a friend in Penn's Manor, a number of anti-slavery persons had a social meeting, and among them was a very beautiful little girl and her father. Mrs. Foster was also present — she is one who has been devoting many years to the cause of the oppressed. With her life in her hand she has faced all the prejudices of the age ; has labored much and suffered much that she might redeem children like you from the curse of slavery.

"The child had been singing, much to the delight of all the company, for she sung very finely. Mrs. Foster saw that she was very fond

of her father; and he, of course, was very
proud of her, as all fathers are of good children.
She called the child to her and engaged her in
conversation. She showed her a picture on an
anti-slavery paper where a child was being sold,
and told her that men made laws in this country
which said little children *might* he sold, and
added, 'I don't know but thy father helps to
make these laws.'

"The child looked very indignant and appeared to feel that he had been accused of a
very vile act. At length she said,

'No! *my* father *don't* make laws to sell little
girls, and he wouldn't let anybody else do it.'

'Go and ask him,' said Mrs. Foster — 'ask
him if he does not *help* to make laws which
allow children to be sold.'

"The child refused. She said she knew her
father didn't do it, and she didn't want to ask
him. But her father told her to do as the lady
wished. She ran to his arms and looking earnestly into his face, said,

"You don't, papa, I *know* you don't make laws
to sell little girls away from their fathers.'

'I suppose I have helped do so,' was the hon-
est confession of the parent.

"The child turned from him in sorrow and humiliation. She was so shocked and so grieved she could make no reply. That father in whose bosom she had ever nestled, and who had always wiped away her tears and made her glad again, was disgraced in her eyes; and for a time she could not feel that he was her father."

"Well," said Charlie, "I guess that father never again helped to make laws to sell children. If our father were so wicked, I don't know what I should do; and Jenie would feel quite as badly as that little girl."

CHAPTER IX.

UNFORTUNATELY for some poor fugitives who were flying from southern bondage, Mrs. Selden's children had an opportunity of witnessing the pro-slavery spirit of their neighbors.

Early one cold frosty morning, Charlie was out trying his sled on some ice and a little newly fallen snow, when his attention was attracted by Cæsar, who was coming across the lot accompanied by a colored man and his wife. On a nearer approach he saw that the woman had in her arms an infant; but such sorrowful, woe-begone countenances he had never seen before. They wore such tattered garments, and had such a weary gait, and such a forlorn appearance, that Charlie concluded they could be none other than slaves; and he was right. They had been directed by a person some miles back to Mr. Selden's, but coming in the evening, and some of the way across the fields, they failed to find his house; and fearing lest they should get among enemies they took refuge under a neighbouring haystack until morning. It was a cold chilly night — a piercing wind and driving sleet had made both man and beast seek their warmest shelter. Think then, my young friends, of the sufferings of these poor creatures, who had no shelter to protect them; and were afraid to enter the abodes of men, lest they should be caught up and thrust back into the prison of southern slavery!

They were warmly welcomed to the fireside of Mr. Selden — parents and children were alike glad to minister to their necessities. It was a long time before feeling was restored to their benumbed limbs; and so completely chilled was the child that they feared it might not survive. The mother seemed nearly frantic at this thought. She used all the remedies prescribed and watched it with the closest attention. When she saw there was but little prospect of its recovery, she pressed it to her bosom and sat in silence. At last the big tear began to fall, and turning to Mrs. Selden, she said,—

"Missis, I've carried this child many a mile, Tom and me; and we both love it dearly, for we've nothing else to love. Poor little thing! Missis, I can't have it die now! Oh, 'its hard to lose the last!"

After a brief space the expression of her countenance changed, and she continued,—

" Missis, I never could bring up this child for old Massa to have for a slave ; and if I had to do that, I'd rather *'twould* die now ! Yes, if you knew what it was to be a slave woman in the South, you'd say so too. Let it die if it must, but, oh God ! save it from being a slave !"

But the child was not doomed to perish thus. Presently it began to recover its concisousness, and in a few hours appeared to be out of danger. Often, in the course of the day, as it lay on its mother's lap, did little Jenie stroke its face, and lay her cheek to its cheek, and say, " They shan't sell it away from its mother. The dogs shan't bite it, and it never shall go and live with those naughty people again."

During all this time, Phil was by no means an uninterested spectator. He was so familiar with Cæsar that he soon got acquainted with Tom, and if I should record all the questions he asked, my young friends would tire of reading them. His principal object seemed to be to find out whether there was any way in which the slaves could revenge themselves upon their masters.

" Why couldn't you get their guns and shoot them ?" said he. " And couldn't you lock them up in their houses, and let them starve ?

"No, little massa," replied Tom, "we don't want to do it. Our freedom is all we ask. Though they have made us very poor and forced us to work when we were sick, and whipped and beaten us, and sold away our children; yet we wish no harm to come upon *them*. If they will make us free, we will never hurt a hair of their heads, but always stand ready to defend them."

This forgiving spirit of Tom's was quite a check to the vindictive disposition of Biddy, who would have recommended that all the punishments ever inflicted upon the slaves be visited upon the masters with seven fold violence. Phil was such a little boy he had no correct idea of slavery, or of the punishments he talked of, but Biddy thought the masters ought to be severely handled, and consequently he said the same.

"See! see!" cried Jenie, as she returned from her mother's drawers and held up a pair of little shoes that Phil had outgrown, "can't the baby wear these? And here is Phil's little wrapper; do put that on the baby, mother, so it never shall get so cold again."

Not many days had elapsed before it was noised abroad that these fugitives were staying at Mr. Selden's, and as it was uncommon for

fugitives to pass that way, it produced considerable excitement. Some pitied the poor creatures
and wished them a happier lot; others manifested no sympathy, and when they heard the slave-
hunter was on their track, they entertained no
fears for their safety ; but on the contrary were
quite willing, not to say anxious, that he should
secure his victims.

These hunters had been prowling about the
neighborhood for a day or two, and one after-
noon they were seen at a public house very near
Mr. Selden's.

Tom and his wife were all unconscious of
their danger; but Cæsar discovered the kidnappers and hastening into the house exclaimed,—

" Run, run, Tom ! for God's sake run !
Woman, take the child and go ! Through the
garden — across the creek — over into the woods.
Away ! away !" he cried, and he swung his
arms and tore around with all the wildness of a
maniac.

" The Lord save us ! ejaculated Biddy, " but
what's the matter with ye, man ; are ye mad ?"

" Here, here !" said Cæsar," put on this overcoat of mine, and button it up tight, and this
hat too, and hold up your head and walk strait

like a man, and never let them know you're a crouching slave."

Mrs. Selden taking the hint, flew to her wardrobe, and brought a good cloak and bonnet for the woman. Tom and his wife were soon ready, and walked off through the garden with all the dignity of a lord and lady.

"But, surely, the terrible man-hunters are not a comin," cried Biday. "It's meself that would break every bone in their skins, should they harm the woman that's laving us, and the darlint babe she carries. What an iligant country this is!" said she scornfully. What quare freedom they have in Ameriky! Niver did I see the likes."

Every inmate of Mr. Selden's house was filled with great anxiety for the fate of the poor wanderers. It was feared that the persons who walked off so leisurely might be suspected of being the slaves in disguise and would be pursued; but they were shortly relieved of this apprehension by the approach of the kidnappers. With the air of desperadoes they entered the back yard and swaggered around the premises muttering curses and threats, and ever and anon casting looks of vengeance at the house.

So fierce and savage did they appear, that even Biddy was awed into silence ; and little Jenie actually shrieked with fear.   At the suggestion of Mrs. Selden, they both retired to the nursery.

Phil stood on a chair at the window, and his great blue eyes grew larger and shone more brightly at every move of the intruders.

" I hope they won't get that baby," said he ; " but, mother, where's my dog ?" and he began to call, " Here Tig ! here Tig ! here Tig !"

Presently the more daring of the two came to the door and gave a violent rap.   Phil scampered off into an adjoining room, but was sure to leave the door ajar so that he could see with one eye all that was going on.   Mrs. Selden was slightly startled at the bold summons, which was immediately succeeded by a rude push that sent the door back against the wall with a slam.   This warned her to collect all her energies.

On the threshold stood a coarse, brutal looking fellow ; his hat cocked on one side, and his overcoat buttoned up, but stretched back in front so as to allow him to thrust both hands into the depths of his pockets.   With a savage leer, he said,—

" I'm told my slaves are here."

"You have been misinformed," replied Mrs. Selden, with quiet dignity.

"But, woman, your neighbors have seen them here. Come! show me where the skulking devils are hid," said he, somewhat in a coaxing way.

Mrs. Selden, feeling indignant at the manner and the request, replied —

"I told you they were not here; but if they were, do you think I would lead a rapacious man-hunter to their hiding place! Do you think I would betray them into the hands of the base miscreant before me! Go home, and seek some more honorable employment than hunting out the stricken and famishing children of oppression, and dragging them back into the vile den of slavery. Begone! unmerciful wretch! let not my threshold be disgraced by contact with such pollution."

The man cowered before the stately bearing and contemptuous tone of Mrs. Selden. He had been accustomed to measure arms with men who gave him offence, but there was something in her earnest rebuke and firm purpose that made him forget his weapons of death; and feeling assured by her manner that the slaves were not there, he and his companion sneaked away to the bar-room from whence they came, and where they found congenial company.

" And where was Cæsar all this time ?" my little readers will ask. Gathered up into the smallest possible compass, and trembling from head to foot like an aspen leaf, he stood in a remote corner of the cellar—a place as dark as midnight. He too had been a slave, altho' he kept it a secret ; and he feared that somebody besides Tom and his wife would be seized as a runaway.

An hour or two after this occurence, Mr. Selden returned, having been necessarily absent the last two days. Learning the foregoing facts, he immediately sent Cæsar to find the fugitives, and directed him to keep them in the woods and take them on to a road some two miles distant, where he would meet them with his carriage. Night had set in and the evening was nearly spent before he was joined by Tom and his wife. He drove on, and on, at a rapid rate : midnight came and passed, and still they pursued their Northern course. The stars began to fade, and ruddy light streak the east ; still they went on.

Quite early in the morning, however, they called at the house of a friend of Mr. Selden. As they drove up, the owner stood in the door. His face beamed with benevolence ; time had silvered his locks, and his once tall and noble form began to feel the weight of years. After a few brief words with Mr. Selden, he told his son George to hitch the horses to the covered dearborn, instead of taking them into the field as he was ready to do.

" But, father, that work *must* be done," observed George.

" Let the plow ever stand in the furrow, and the corn rot on the ear, rather than I should fail in my duty to God's suffering poor !" replied the parent.

George did as ordered. The slaves got into the dearborn ; the old man taking the reins followed, and after a breakfast was handed in to Tom and his wife, they departed.

This kind friend took them on some fifteen or twenty miles, and placed them in charge of another, who continued the same course northward, and by changing hands a good many times and walking a long distance, they at length reached Canada in safety.

THE FUGITIVE'S SONG.

We're away, we're away, and bend gladly the oar
To the heart-cheering sound of Niagara's roar ;
For a fate worse than death would be ours should we stay;
So to Canada's borders we hasten away.

We come from the plains of the sunny South-west,
Where the Earth in her beautiful garment is drest ;
And where all would be fair, did not slavery's hand
Scatter mildew, and blighting, and wo o'er the land.

Then away, then away o'er the foam-crested wave
To Britannia's home for the fugitive slave ;
Where the Lion of England keeps ever at bay
The prowling man hunter who seeks for his prey.

And though long have our spirits been weary and sad,
Thy anthem, Niagara, maketh us glad :
And we read in the beautiful bow on thy spray,
A promise of safety and freedom to-day.

Then away, then away, and ply cheerly the oar,
Each stroke brings us nearer to Canada's shore.
We are there! we are there! our boat touches the strand,
And the bow of our vessel is high on the land.

Unship every oar, for our labor is done,
Our freedom is gained, and our manhood is won!
The toils we endured, and the dangers, are past!
We are *free*! we are FREE, we are FREE then at last!

B. S. J.

CHAPTER X.

In the course of a few days the excitement attendant upon the events mentioned in the last chapter subsided; but they left a lasting impression upon the minds of the young Seldens. The appearance of the fugitives among them deepened their interest in the condition of the bondman; and made them hate slavery more than they had ever done befoie. They tired not in hearing of the slave, and the mother ceased not to instruct them.

"I have many things yet, my dear children, to tell you," said she; " indeed I have but just begun to expose the horrors of the great prison house. The workings of slavery, however, in all their details you could not comprehend; and I suppose you could form no correct idea of the amount of vice, and the deep degradation produced by this system.

"I have spoken to you of cruelties, the thought of which seems to make you shudder; yet these same cruelties, the whipping and branding, the starving and burning, are the least objectionable part of slavery. Probably you will not be able to understand this now; but when you grow older you will know better what I mean. The human mind, that part of man that thinks, and reasons, and plans, and embraces truth, and struggles to rise above the earthly things that surround it, is of far more worth than the body that is doomed to perish. But in slavery the mind fares worse even than the body. It cannot rise — it is kept in darkness — it is forbidden to expand, or catch a glimpse of the light and knowledge that prevail. I remember, Charlie, that you felt very badly last summer when you found out that Wm. O'Rafferty could not read."

"Well, mother, I like so well to have new books, and know how to read them, and to study geography, and history, and to learn something about the world and the people who live in it, I pity one so ignorant as William was."

"He was ignorant," replied the mother, "because his parents did not send him to school. They could have done so had they wished, but every school in the land is closed against three millions of American slaves! They are spurned from the threshold of every institution of learning; and an attempt even to learn to read the name of God is punished as a crime! If books had never been made, and the art of printing was unknown, the slave would be just as wise as he is now. Oh! it is dreadful to keep a man in such darkness and blindness — to hide from his view all knowledge and science, the discoveries of present and past ages — to shut out the beautiful truths of the gospel, and keep him as ignorant as the beasts of the field. This is far, far worse than to have the body beaten and bruised."

" Why do they keep them in ignorance ?" inquired Charlie. " They could work just as well if they knew more."

" If they did not keep them in ignorance they could not keep them in slavery — people who are enlightened can't be enslaved."

" Well," said Jenie, " if I was there I'd teach the little girls their A B C's."

" My dear one !" replied the parent, " they would punish my little daughter very severely for this kind act, if they thought she was old enough to understand the law against it."

" But I would teach them when nobody saw me — after the folks had all gone to bed."

" The overseer might be up though," returned her mother. " He is often sneaking about the negro quarters in the night, and peeking into the cabins to see if anything is going on contrary to plantation rules. The slaves, and all who are supposed to be their friends, are watched in all their movements, and every offence promptly punished. The slaveholders will allow no information to be given, nor anything said to make the slaves discontented.

" Should I go to Louisiana and tell the poor creatures that they ought not to be compelled to work without wages, and that they have as good a right to liberty as their masters, although they knew this before, yet my words would doubtless make them more dissatisfied, and for that offence I thould be thrown into a prison. I should be separated from my family and shut up with pickpockets and murderers. My heart, I think, would be very sad; perhaps I should grow pale and poor, and be so worn and wasted that when I came out my dear children would not know me.

" Or should I carry there," she continued, " any papers or pamphlets against slavery, and distribute them among the people; if calculated to produced disobedience among the slaves— and all such papers would if the slaves knew what they contained—I should be sentenced to imprisonment at hard labor for life, or suffer death at the discretion of the court. Yes, if I was not hung at once or killed in some other way, so long as I lived my only home would be within the cold walls of a prison ; and I should have to labor daily under the eye of a task-master."

The thought of their mother being treated thus, made the children look sorrowful ; but Charlie bethought him of the instruction she had given, and said —

" But that wouldn't be equal to what the slaves have to suffer."

" That's very true," she replied, " and I am glad that you understand that imprisonment for life is better than slavery."

" But it's quare enough, mistress," cried Biddy, "to bring such a black trouble upon a body, and shut him up like a thief, or break his neck as if he had done murder, when he's guilty of nothin at all, at all. For sure, mistress, it's no crime to talk or write agin slavery; the Holy Mother would niver smile upon him that should hould his pace."

" It *is* strange, Biddy, and very wicked too, but the slaveholders are determined to maintain

their system; and therefore they threaten, and
treat with the greatest severity all the abolitionists they can get hold of. They used to say
that slavery should not be talked about among
them; and a South Carolina paper once declared that the man who should attempt to speak
of its evils with a view to its overthrow, in that
same moment should have his tongue cut out
and cast away.

"A Georgia paper, speaking of an abolitionist
once, said, 'He ought to have been hung as high
as Haman, and left to rot on the gibbet until the
wind whistled through his bones! The cry of
the whole South should be *death*, INSTANT DEATH
to the abolitionist wherever he is caught!'

"The general sentiment of southern papers
has been, that slavery is deep rooted among
them, and *shall* remain forever; and he who
speaks against it is fit only for the halter. The
acts of violence committed upon abolitionists by
slaveholders and their abettors would fill many
a volume.

"It is not two years, since Charles T. Torrey
died in a prison for no act but that of delivering
the oppressed from the hand of their tyrant
masters. He went where slavery existed and

witnessed the hopeless condition of its victims.
He saw then truly that they had fallen among
thieves — they were stripped and wounded —
they were bleeding and groaning under the
weight of the burdens imposed upon them.
They cried for deliverance but there was none
to help! The people all around were enemies
and determined to prolong their captivity. They
were bowed down under a load of sorrow —
affliction such as seldom falls to the lot of man,
was theirs. The worst forms of heathenism,
the deepest ignorance had settled down upon
their moral being — the world was to them a
vast desert, lighted up by scarcely a ray of joy,
or hope, or comfort.

"Mr. Torrey was moved with pity, as every
body would be who had a heart to feel. He
had read in his Bible these commandments,
'Open the prison doors to them that are bound,'
'Break every yoke and let the oppressed go
free,' 'Deliver him that is spoiled from the
hands of the spoiler.' He endeavored to obey
these precepts by assisting slaves to escape from
the power of the oppressor. He succeeded in
a great many cases; and the name of Charles
T. Torrey will ever be remembered with the

deepest gratitude, by many an emancipated slave who now treads the free soil of Canada, happy in the consciousness of his liberty, and in the possession of his wife and little ones.

"But at length he was detected in his work of mercy and confined in a loathesome jail. After two years of suffering — and years are very long in a prison where one is shut out from all who love or care for him — he attempted to escape. For this he was loaded with heavy irons and placed in a cold cell. His fate then was hard indeed — severe pain and sickness came upon him and he got neither rest, nor sleep, nor comfort. The long days passed slowly away, and it seemed to him that the nights would never end. Oh! how he needed the kindness and care of his family; but they could not be with him to minister to his wants. He desired to see the faces of those he loved; he longed to hear the voice of some kind friend; but the stillness of his gloomy cell was broken only by his groans and the clanking of the chain that bound him."

"But, mother, didn't his little children want to see him?" asked Jenie.

"Yes, dear. His little Charles and Mary

greatly desired his return. They felt, I suppose, just as you would feel should your father
be taken away and shut up in jail. They
missed him every where; they felt that the
family circle was broken. When they came
to the table they saw his vacant place; when
they kneeled with their mother at morning and
evening prayer, the absent father ever came up
before them. The voice of him they loved was
heard no more in their midst; and they anxious-
ly inquired, 'When will father come?'"

"*Did* he never come again?" inquired Jenie.

"No, my child, he was sentenced to six years
hard labor in a penitentiary. Many efforts were
made to clear him at his trial, and also to secure
a pardon after his sentence, but they were all in
vain. He was doomed to fall a victim to that
law which forbids man to obey God; for six
years, or two years even, of confinement and
labor, added to what he had already suffered,
were more than he could endure. Oh! it was
hard to die in that cheerless abode far away
from home and friends, and have none save an
officer of the law to listen to his last words and
smoothe his dying pillow.

"Less than eighteen months after this sentence, word went abroad that Charles T. Torrey was no more; and when his children asked again 'When will father come?' the reply was, *Never!* NEVER! His eyes are closed in death, and his voice silenced in the stillness of the tomb."

"Then the little children have no father," said Jenie, thoughtfully.

"No," returned the mother, "slaveholders have robbed them of their father, and left their mother very sad and sorrowful."

"Did they ever try to treat others in that way?" inquired Charlie.

"Yes, a great many have suffered at their hands. Wm. Lloyd Garrison, the man who first roused this guilty nation by declaring that the slave ought to have his liberty immediately and unconditionally, was once imprisoned in the same jail where Mr. Torrey suffered so much; and the great State of Georgia has, for the last fifteen years, been offering a reward of FIVE THOUSAND DOLLARS to any person who would place him in the power of the slaveholders, that he might be murdered as Charles T. Torrey was murdered.

"Very many have been imprisoned," continued Mrs. Selden. "Calvin Fairbanks is now in a Kentucky penitentiary ; and he has got to live and labor there fifteen long years from the time he was put in, unless death comes to his relief, and all because he was merciful to the slave.

"Jonathan Walker, of Massachusetts, was imprisoned in Florida — placed in a pillory, and had the letters S. S. burned into the palm of his right hand with a red hot branding iron, and all because he turned not a deaf ear to the cry of the perishing bondman."

"What were the letters S. S. for ?" inquired the boy.

"Slave Stealer, they were designed for."

"But he didn't steal slaves, did he ? rejoined Charlie.

"Just as much as your father stole Tom and his wife the other day — they both helped slaves to escape from their masters.

"The Southerners are roused to fury at the least movement on the part of any to destroy slavery. So angry do they become, that their ravings are like the ravings of madmen. A southern woman once said of Arthur Tappan of New York, ' I could cut his throat from ear to ear.' "

"Niver did I hear the like," cried Biddy. "Bould work that for a woman to be after doing. I'd like to show her the strength that's in me. I'd teach her better manners than to talk of cutting a man's throat bekase he spake agin slavery."

"I am sorry to hear you talk so much about fighting, Biddy," said Mrs. Selden; "a fighting spirit is no better than the spirit of slavery. You must try to be more gentle and forgiving. I am afraid my children will catch your warlike disposition, and forget the peace principles I have taught them."

"Well, mistress, I beg pardon if what I've been spaking be wrong. But what ye've been telling us is enough to stir the heart that's in a body, and make every drop of blood spake out. The blessed St. Patrick himself, although he was a saint, would have been as full of fight as meself maybe; and there's not an Irish lad of spirit but would be ready to give the ould thieves a taste of his shillalah. Though 'taint very pacable like, the feelin would come up in me that I'd like to try them a bit myself."

CHAPTER XI.

Charlie did not often wait for his mother to commence the conversation about the slaves and their friends; but he generally opened the subject himself by asking questions.

"I was thinking," said he, "from what you told us the other day, that some abolitionists had, after all, been treated almost as badly as the slaves."

"Slaveholders," replied the mother, "are as cruel to them as they well can be, but it is not in their power to injure them so deeply as they injure the slaves."

"Well, I shouldn't like to live in the South. I don't suppose any body would care what such a young boy as I am would say; but when I grow to be a man, I shall do all I can for the slaves, and if I lived there they might put me in prison or kill me. Mother, I *am* glad that we live here in the North where we can say what we please about slavery, and do as much as we like to help fugitives."

"But are you quite sure, Charlie, that we *can* say what we please, and do what we like?"

"Why, can't we?" said he.

" No! Should any one choose to prosecute your father for harboring Tom and his wife who were here last week, and for carrying them off beyond the reach of the hunters, they could fine him FIVE HUNDRED DOLLARS ; and should he refuse to pay it, he might be imprisoned."

" Why, mother! I did not think there *was* such a law. How did father dare to do it ?"

" He dares to disregard all laws that interfere with our duty toward our fellow men," observed the parent. " It is our duty to feed the hungry— Tom and his wife were nearly starved. It is our duty to clothe the naked—Tom and his wife were covered only with rags, and any laws which forbid us to do these things, we should no more be forced to obey than our hands could be bound with a spider's web. If men choose to punish us for such acts we are ready to suffer. It is our duty to ' Hide the outcast '; therefore did we secrete Tom and his wife, and convey them away from their enemies."

" Oh ! that's what it means to 'Hide the outcast,' is it ?" cried Charlie. " Then the slaves are outcast, are they ?"

" Yes, child, there are no people to whom the word would better apply, for there are none so

poor—none so afflicted—none so cruelly cast
out from the regard and fellowship of men and
the joys of life as the slave."

"Now I can tell Jenie what it means to 'Hide
the outcast.' You needn't do it, mother; let me.
You remember she wanted to know once. But
I guess this law against hiding the outcast is only
just to frighten people—nobody ever was taken
up for doing such a thing?" said he inquiringly.

"Yes, it has been done many times; and so
far from being free to speak as we please a-
gainst slavery, the greatest violence has been
used upon the abolitionists—their property has
been destroyed—their meetings broken up—their
persons injured, and life has been sacrificed."

"What! not by northern men, mother?"

"Yes, and by men who call themselves gentlemen and christians. I have already told you
that the people of the North are no better than
slaveholders; indeed they *are* the slaveholders.
They don't claim the slaves as their property,
and get the benefit of their labor, it is true; but
they uphold the master in his wickedness, and
stand ready to aid him to retain his victims
whenever their services are needed.

"Let me make it plain to you. Supposing

Edward Miller should take away all your books, and playthings, and good clothes, and make you work very hard and earn money so that he could have it to spend ; and suppose his father, who is a very large, strong man, should stand by and see his son's conduct, and if you attempted to escape should seize you, and put you back again into the power of Edward ; and if you refused to submit to his authority, the father should threaten to shoot you ; whom would you blame most, Mr. Miller or Edward ?"

"I should blame Mr. Miller most," was the prompt reply," for Ned couldn't treat me in that way without help.   We often wrestle at school, and I am always an overmatch for him."

" Very well.   Now Mr. Miller would stand in the same relation to you, that the North stands to the slaves.   *They* are an overmatch for their masters ; and were it not for the aid of northern men they would get their freedom to-morrow.   Many a · slave have I heard say, ' Leave us alone with our masters, and we'll take care of them !   It is the interference of the North we dread — it is the northern people that keep us in our chains."

" But, mother, the northern men don't threaten

to shoot the slaves if they don't obey their masters."

"Certainly they do. It is but a short time since that Mr. Wilmot, a distinguished member of Congress from Pennsylvania, declared in a great convention, that should the slaves rise up and resist the outrages committed upon them, he would go down to the South and shed the last drop of his blood, if necessary, to put them down and bring them into subjection again. He said he would sacrifice his life in order to maintain the system.

"So you see, Charlie, if the slaves *should* make an effort to throw off the oppression they are laboring under — should they say, God gave us a right to liberty and we will maintain it — we will be free — we will no longer suffer violence upon our wives and daughters — our little children shall never be torn from our arms and sold away — we will work no longer without just compensation; should the slaves rise up and say *these* things, the military force of the South would be called out, and with musket and cannon they would threaten to shoot every man who would not surrender. But if the slaves still maintained their ground, and were determined to be free ; if the threats and curses, the smoke and blaze, and roar of guns, and the groans of their dying companions who were falling all around them did not induce them to yield ; if they still said, we *will* have liberty or death, then Mr. Wilmot, and those who feel like him, would go down and compel the famishing and wretched victims of American despotism to submit their necks again to the yoke of slavery. He might be gratified by bathing his glittering bayonet in the heart's blood of men who were struggling to be free — whose only crime was that of endeavoring to break the chain of tyranny."

" I hope there are not many men like Mr. Wilmot," observed Charlie.

" There are not many who would *say* what Mr. Wilmot has said, but there are very many who would do what he said he would do. Indeed, it is required by the supreme law of the land that they shall do it ; and northern men have entered into an agreement with southern men that they will do it ; and every year they renew the promise they have made."

" Every time we talk about the slaves, mother, you make their case worse and worse.

Why, what a condition they *are* in! The very
thought of it makes me shudder. They are
treated so cruelly where they are; and when
they try to get away they are often caught and
carried back; and when they rise up and try to
be free, men all over the country stand ready to
shoot them. I don't believe any poor creatures
ever *were* treated so badly before. Why don't
the folks talk about it, and try to do something
for them? I should think ministers would
preach on the subject.

"Some of them do. Now and then one
preaches the doctrines of liberty, and brings
up the wrongs and sufferings of the oppressed
before the people, and rebukes them for their
indifference and their support of the system;
but generally they talk only in favor of slavery.
They are as much interested in sustaining it as
any other class of persons; and a great many
actually hold slaves, and beat, and drive, and
starve, and hunt them, just as the worst of slaveholders do."

"What! ministers, mother! Do ministers
hold slaves. I shouldn't think anybody would
want to hear them preach. Why I thought
they were all christians. You never told me

much about them, but I've heard the boys say that their mothers told *them* they must remember what the ministers said, for they were good men; and little Mary Fisher, when she was here yesterday, said when her mother put her to bed, she often asked her to repeat what she could that the minister said the Sunday before, and told her she must always remember it, for he was a man of God."

"I suppose she had reference to Mr. Perkins," returned the mother, "and he does say a great many things that ought to be remembered; but so far from doing his duty to the slaves, he is one of the most violent opposers the abolitionists have. He says that slavery is *right* and ought to exist; and that they who talk against it are fools, fanatics, and infidels. There is not a tyrant on a southern plantation that has more of the spirit of slavery than he; and there are scores of others, both ministers and church members, who are just like him. They profess to do as they would be done by, then bind, or help to bind their own brethren and sisters in the church with the strong cord of slavery— strike down all their rights, and turn their sources of happiness into fountains of grief and misery. The society and affection of my dear husband and children make *me* very joyous; but these professed christians make the slave woman mourn that she ever had a husband; they make her regret the day her children were born. Instead of taking pleasure in loving her friends, they make her wish that she had no love, and that all the sources of her tenderness were dried up; then would she be saved the extreme agony of separation from the objects of her affection. After her husband is torn away she is forced to live with another; and thus at the will of the master she is married and unmarried as many times as he chooses. The exceeding sinfulness of this you will understand better as you grow older. It destroys the pure and holy relation of husband and wife, for he whom the slave woman calls her husband to-day may be the husband of another to-morrow, so there is no lawful marriage among them; and this is the cause of untold vice and immorality. This, you understand, is the fault of the system and those who sustain it, and not the fault of the slaves.

" The most horrible treatment I ever read of, has been that received by these oppressed people at the hands of professors of religion. Frederick Douglass, who was once a slave, says he ' ever found *them* the meanest and the basest, the most cowardly and cruel of all masters.' Any crime that other slaveholders are guilty of, they certainly do not hesitate to commit."

"Then they are not christians, are they?" inquired Charlie. "You have taught me that a christian was one who spent his life in doing good — in trying to make the people around him better and happier. A christian, you said, always loved his fellow men, and never meant to do them any injury — he looked upon them all as his brothers and sisters, so he could not harm them. You have often said we all had one Father who was called God, who made us all, and this beautiful world too, and every thing that exists, and that we could best show our love and gratitude to this Father by loving each other. I remember that, for you told me also there was no way in which I could please *my* father so well as in loving and being very kind to my little brother and my dear sister Jenie."

"I am glad you remember the lesson so well," replied the mother; "and in regard to slaveholders being christians, I think you can

judge for yourself. Mrs. Weld, who was a
native and for a long time a resident of South
Carolina, knew a presbyterian woman in the
city of Charleston, who had a young girl so
unmercifully whipped that large pieces of flesh
were actually cut out of her back. Mrs. Weld
saw the girl, and she said she could have laid
her whole finger in the gashes. Did that woman
love the girl, Charlie, and had she the spirit of
a christian ?"

"No, mother, she hated her, and I should
think she was more of a Turk than a Christian."

"The Rev. Francis Hawley tells us of a
presbyterian minister who whipped a slave very
cruelly, and then nearly drowned him, and
finally fastened him into a corner of a fence
between the rails, and kept him there so long
that he died a few days after. He tells also of
a methodist minister who had a slave that was
suspected of knowing that some others were
going to rise and try to get their liberty; and on
that suspicion merely, he was hung up like a
dog and left to die. Mr. Hawley states that he
himself, although a baptist minister, had been
out with rifle and dogs to hunt down flying fugitives. I might mention hundreds of similar

cases. Did those ministers treat their fellow men kindly, and try to do them good, my son ?"

" Why, no! of course not ; they tried to do them all the harm they could. They did not treat them as though they were their brothers at all. But, mother, do these ministers preach, and pray, and sing like other ministers ?"

" Yes, and those who whip hardest, and whose lash cuts deepest, are often those who sing and shout the loudest and pray the longest. That Charleston woman I spoke of, used to pray three times a day ; and once every day, and often three times, did some one of the servants of her house receive a scourging. Sometimes they were beaten, as in one case Mrs. Weld mentioned, till the blood gushed from the mouth and nose and ears of the sufferer."

" Why are they whipped so much ? I am sure they must do wrong in some way."

" Sometimes there would seem to be a pretty good reason for punishment, if punishments are ever justifiable ; but often the slightest mistake, such as spilling a cup of tea, or burning a piece of toast, causes the offender to be treated in the most brutal manner. John Graham, of Massachusetts, describes a scene that he witnessed at a breakfast table in South Carolina, or rather on an island near by.

"The servant happened to pour a little more molasses on the plate of a child than it usually had. Her master was angry, rose from the table, and took both of her hands in one of his, and with the other, beat her first on one side of the head, and then on the other as long as his hand could endure it. Then he took off his shoe and with the heel began in the same manner as with his hand. Finally the woman raised her elbow to ward off the blows; for which he called a stout negro to hold her hands behind her. This being done, he renewed his blows until they became intolerable, and she fell upon the floor and screamed for help and mercy. After she fell he continued to beat her, and Mr. Graham thought she would die in his hands. She got up, however, went out and washed off the blood, and came in again before they arose from the table. Then she was a pitiable object indeed. Her ears were three or four times as thick as usual, her eyes awfully blood-shotten, her lips, nose, chin, and whole head so swollen that no one would have known her; and for all this she had to say 'Thank you, massa.'"

"What a shocking story!" cried Charlie. "Why, mother, you will make me feel that every body is bad, and that there are no good people in the world. The people in the south are slave-holders and friends of slavery ; and the people of the North, although they don't own slaves, help to hold them, which is just as bad; so I am sure there can't be any good folks in this country at least."

"Oh, yes, Charlie, there are many good people. All ministers and church members are not like those I have spoken of, though there are a multitude who are no better and many who are worse; yet there are some good people among them who are doing what they can for the poor and the distressed, and for the cause of human liberty. There are a great many abolitionists who are laboring faithfully and earnestly for the redemption of the bondman."

"Are all abolitionists christians ?" asked Charlie.

"No, I do not call them so. They are good as far as their hatred for slavery goes, but some of them do not seem inclined to carry out the principles of love and kindness toward those around them, as well as toward the slave. Such do not appear to me to be christians altogether."

CHAPTER XII.

"You said the other day," observed Mrs. Selden to Charlie, " that a slaveholding woman we were speaking of, was more of a Turk than a christian. The religion of the Turks, which is Mahomedan, does not allow them to hold in bondage one who is a Mahomedan also. The moment he professes to believe in that religion, he is no longer a slave ; but in this country slaves join the same churches with their masters, and they are slaves still. The yoke of bondage is made no lighter, the scourging no less, the years of suffering no fewer. It was once well said by Wendell Phillips, of Boston, 'It would be better for the slaves of America if we should all wake up Turks to-morrow morning, instead of professed christians.' "

" Do *tell* me," said Charlie, " how these slaves are ever going to get their liberty. I don't see that they ever can be free."

" I trust they will," replied the mother. "I feel assured that the progress of human liberty in the world, and the agitation of the slavery question in this country, will at length effect their deliverance. We cannot tell how soon this time will come — it may be nearer than we think for ; and it may be very distant. Great progress toward their liberation has already been made. Slavery is far less defended now than formerly. 'Tis but a few years since that abolitionists could hardly have a peaceable meeting. Their assembling was a signal for all the rowdies in the country round about to collect clubs, and stones, and brickbats, and eggs, and burst in upon the meeting and hurl these missiles at the speaker and his friends."

"What! people here in the North do that? Well, they were only rowdies, and rowdies are always ready for anything," observed Charlie.

"There were many, my son, engaged in these mobs that would not like to be called rowdies. There were merchants and doctors, lawyers and ministers, deacons and elders that gave countenance to, and assisted in these disgraceful scenes. Those were not the most guilty who threw the stones and the eggs, for they would not have done it had not others, calling themselves gentlemen, urged them on ; had not ministers justified slavery, and talked and preached against the abolitionists ; and had not professing christians said the abolitionists ought to be put down. It was these who were most to blame."

" Was any body ever injured or killed at these times, mother?"

" Yes, a great many have been seriously injured, and some have lost their lives. Many have been severely beaten — stones and brickbats thrown by madmen are very apt to hurt. Abolitionists have been taken off at night into the woods, covered with tar and feathers, and otherwise treated in a most brutal manner, and then left there in an exhausted and suffering condition. Anti-slavery printing presses have been seized, dragged away and thrown into a neighboring river, there to rust beneath its waters. Private houses have been forced open and their furniture brought out and burned in the public street. Elijah P. Lovejoy was pursued many a time by a ruthless mob and finally murdered. Five rifle balls were lodged in his body, and he fell a bleeding corpse. His enemies, who were the friends of slavery, rejoiced that the voice of one more defender of liberty was hushed forever.

" Meeting houses have been burned, and temples dedicated to liberty reduced to ashes.

When we go to Philadelphia again, I will show you the spot where stood Pennsylvania Hall, one of the most beautiful public buildings in that city. It was erected by the friends of the slave, and was the first hall in the country ever dedicated to free discussion. When the building was completed, the advocates of liberty assembled from all parts of the northern States to consecrate it to the God of Freedom. But the spirit of slavery was roused. On the first and second days of the meeting threats of violence were boldly uttered, and ere the third had closed, the Hall was surrounded by a mob who yelled, and hooted, and hissed, and broke in the windows and committed acts of personal outrage. On the evening of the fourth day they set it on fire. Dense volumes of smoke burst from the doors and windows, the red flames lighted up the dark sky, and in a few hours only the crumbling and blackened walls remained to tell of the vile deed that slavery's defenders had done."

" It seems to me there is no safety in this country for anybody who tries to do right," observed Charlie." For keeping fugitives they can be fined or imprisoned, when holding meetings they are mobbed, their property destroyed, their

public houses burned, and they themselves beat-
en, and tarred, and killed, and all because they
want to make the slaves free, and stop men from
robbing them and selling away their children.
Why, mother, it is horrible! I should think that
such things would not be allowed, even among
savages, who are very ignorant and wicked."

"Such things," replied the mother, "would
disgrace savages, and how much more disgraceful are they in this nation which claims to be the
only free nation on earth, and professes to be
better, more enlightened, more truly christian than
any other. The fact that the United States hold
three millions of slaves, proves that the people
are neither christians nor lovers of liberty. Their
professions are a hollow mockery, and render
them subject to the disgust, and censure, and
ridicule of the whole world. Those who make
the highest professions of good-will to all, are
the very persons who rivet the chains of slavery
upon the necks of starving, heart-broken, and
sorrowing men and women. Many who stand
up in the pulpit and say God ordained *them* to
preach, say also that slavery is not sinful, and
ought not to be overthrown. It is the influence
of such men, added to the power of guns and

bayonets, that keeps the slaves where they are. Indeed, I doubt whether guns and bayonets would be used, were not their use sanctioned by the ministers and the church. They say that it is right—they themselves use them; and thus, by the words and example of those who profess to be christians, are the people made easy in their sins, and continue to hold in bondage those whom they ought to love, and labor to benefit. Nothing stands so much in the way of giving freedom to those in bonds, as the churches which defend slavery, and oppose all the efforts of the abolitionists."

"I suppose abolitionists have nothing to do with such churches," returned Charlie. "But tell me, mother, if there are such bloody mobs now-a-days as there used to be?"

"No! I was going to say that there are a great many encouraging things at the present time. Meetings are not often broken up now, and slavery is talked about every where — in the North, at least — in public and in private, in churches, in political meetings, and in social gatherings. You can scarcely take up a news-paper but has something in it against slavery; it is to be regretted, however, that so much is published in favor of it; still the tone of the press is very different from what it was. For sixteen years have the abolitionists been scattering their papers, and tracts and pamphlets throughout the land ; they have sent abroad their speakers, both men and women, who have gone to and fro among the people telling of the wrongs and oppressions of the slave, and calling upon those who loved justice and mercy to aid in his deliverance. The happy results of this agitation are now seen ; the rebukes, the reasonings, the appeals of these laborers have been abundantly prospered. Thousands and tens of thousands have been led to see that slavery is a sin ; political parties have been distracted and weakened by the discussion of this question ; many have withdrawn from them, and their leaders begin to see that it is necessary to do, or pretend to do something in favor of liberty.

" This agitation has affected the churches in a still greater degree — their holiness has been shown to be mere pretence, and their love of self and sect greater than their love of truth and righteousness. Those who really desire to do right, have been made to feel, that that is not a christian church whose members bind, and rob, and bruise their equal brethren. Thousands have left these churches as well as the parties, and proclaimed to the world that they will no longer remain with those who support slavery.

"Even a change has been effected in the South, which was formerly so bitter, and so determined not to hear. The truth has been forced upon the slaveholders, and here and there one has given freedom to all those he held in captivity. A willingness to hear this subject discussed has gradually increased among them, and especially is this true of Western Virginia and Kentucky. In the latter State an anti-slavery paper has been established which is read with interest by hundreds of slaveholders, and tells mightily on the cause of human freedom.

"Prejudice against a colored skin, which has so deeply injured the black man both at the South and at the North, is giving way before a more enlightened and christian feeling. It has excluded colored children from our schools and colleges, it has driven men and women from the cabins of our steamboats, and thrust them upon the deck, no matter how cold or unpleasant the weather."

"But, mother, I don't understand you; did'nt

the white people want them to sit in the cabin ?"

" No, they said they couldn't bear the presence of a negro. I knew one woman who was traveling on a boat, who sickened and died in consequence of being turned out of the cabin and being exposed to the night air on the deck of a steamer. This prejudice has compelled colored people to ride in an inferior car on railroads, and entirely excluded them from stage coaches in various places. It has set apart for them an obscure corner of the church, called the ' Negro Pew '; for the religion of this land is so full of hatred to the colored man, that it will not permit him to sit with his white brother, even in the house of prayer. The abolitionists have succeeded to some extent in convincing the people that this prejudice is anti-christian, and they have themselves set the example of treating the colored man as an equal. The result has been, that many of the schools in the North admit colored children the same as white ; colored people are much less frequently driven from the cabins of our steam-boats and excluded from railroad cars ; the churches are begining to be ashamed of their ' Negro Pews', and to admit that all men are brethren and should treat each other as such.

These things encourage us to believe that the cruel reign of slavery is drawing to a close.

" We should think the slave's deliverance close at hand, were not his oppressors adding extensive territory to their domains, and waging an infamous war with Mexico in order to extend and perpetuate the system."

" What territory have they added, mother, and why can they hold on to their slaves any longer by fighting the Mexicans ?"

" The masters were afraid their slaves would escape into Texas, a province belonging to Mexico, and adjoining our southern border; consequently they seized upon it, and re-established slavery, which Mexico had abolished nearly twenty years ago, and finally added it to the United States.   You know that men who take children from their mothers, would not hesitate to steal land from their neighbors.   As might be supposed, many difficulties grew out of this, and as the Mexicans do not so well understand the art of war and are a much less powerful people than those of the United States, the latter sent down their soldiers, who destroyed their forts, captured their cities, murdered their men and women, and even killed little children who could do them no harm. Thousands have been murdered and wounded in this war, and hundreds of bodies have been left to rot, and taint the air; and all because the slaveholder wanted more power and more territory in order that slavery might live forever."

" The abolitionists certainly have a great work before them yet — very much remains to be done, although a great deal has been accomplished. Many have united in the work which was commenced by a very few. Where there was one in former days to labor for the slave there are now hundreds, and a great many little boys and girls like you and Jenie are helping in the work. If we all do what we can, and try to get others to do what they can, I think it will not be many years before slavery shall be no more; and the happy faces of the slave children, and their gay and joyous laugh, will be a pleasant sight and sweet music to those who aided in making them and their parents free."

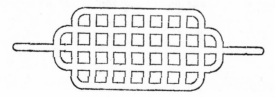

FREEDOM'S GATHERING.

A summons is spoken, the land is awake
And free hearts have gathered from ocean to lake.
The cause we engage in is spotless and pure,
And the triumph we seek shall forever endure.

Though tyrants denounce, and pursue us with ill,
Our hearts shall be faithful to liberty still.
Then rally, then rally, come one and come all ;
'Tis for Truth and for Freedom we echo the call.

Thy hill-tops, New England, have leaped at the cry,
And the far spreading West and the South give reply ;
It has rolled o'er the land till the farthermost glen
Re-echos the summons again and again.

Oppression has heard in his temple of blood,
And reads on it's wall the hand writing of God ;
Niagara's torrent has thundered it forth,
And it burns in the sentinel star of the North.

It is seen in the lightning, it speaks in the thunder,
And slavery's fetters are breaking asunder ;
Ere long will the captive's deliverance be won,
And our country her beautiful garments put on.

Then on to the conflict for Freedom and Truth !
Come Matron, come Maiden, come Manhood and Youth!
Come gather, come gather, come one, and come all !
And soon shall the altar of slavery fall.

The forests shall know it, and lift up their voice
To bid the green prairies and vallies rejoice ;
And the " Father of Waters " join Mexico's sea,
In the anthem of Nature for millions set free.

B. S. J.